Annotated Bibliography of Publications from the U.S. Navy's Marine Mammal Program

Forrest G. Wood

NIMBLE BOOKS LLC: THE AI LAB FOR BOOK-LOVERS
~ FRED ZIMMERMAN, EDITOR ~
Humans and AI making books richer, more diverse, and more surprising.

Publishing Information

(c) 2023 Nimble Books LLC
ISBN: 978-1-60888-267-0

AI-generated Keyword Phrases

marine mammals; dolphins; whales; anatomy and physiology; auditory system; echolocation abilities; sound production; reception; target detection; discrimination; navigation; communication; sensory capabilities; diving behavior; reproductive biology; physiological adaptations; biology; behavior; health; study methods; management techniques ; distribution ; abundance ; migration patterns ; general behavior ; sound production ; bowhead whales ; gray whales ; feeding patterns ; habitat preferences ; marine mammal trainers selection ; capture and adaptation of beluga whales ; cytogenetic studies

Publisher's Notes

This annotated edition illustrates the capabilities of the AI Lab for Book-Lovers to add context and ease-of-use to manuscripts. It includes five types of abstracts, building from simplest to more complex: TLDR (one word), ELI5, TLDR (vanilla), Scientific Style, and Action Items; three essays to increase viewpoint diversity: Grounds for Dissent, Red Team Critique, and MAGA Perspective; and Notable Passages and Nutshell Summaries for each page.

ANNOTATIONS

- **Publishing Information** ii
- **AI-generated Keyword Phrases** ii
- **Publisher's Notes** ii
- **Abstracts** iv
  - TL;DR (one word) iv
  - Explain It To Me Like I'm Five Years Old iv
  - TL;DR (vanilla) iv
  - Scientific Style iv
  - Action Items v
- **Visual Abstracts** vi
  - Moods vi
- **Viewpoints** vii
  - Grounds for Dissent vii
  - Red Team Critique viii
  - MAGA Perspective ix
- **Page-by-Page Summaries** xi
- **Notable Passages** xvii

ABSTRACTS

TL;DR (ONE WORD)

Marine mammals.

EXPLAIN IT TO ME LIKE I'M FIVE YEARS OLD

This document is a collection of papers and reports about dolphins and whales. It talks about how they can hear and make sounds, and how they use those sounds to find things and talk to each other. It also talks about their bodies and how they are adapted to live in the water. The document also has information about where these animals live, how they move around, and what they eat. It even talks about how scientists study and take care of them. There are also some other topics like how people

TL;DR (VANILLA)

This document contains research papers and reports on various topics related to marine mammals, focusing on dolphins and whales. It covers their anatomy, echolocation abilities, sound production, target detection, navigation, communication, sensory capabilities, diving behavior, reproductive biology, and other adaptations. It also includes information on the distribution and behavior of bowhead whales and gray whales. Additionally, it discusses topics such as marine mammal trainers' selection process, beluga whale capture and adaptation methods, porpoise cytogenetic studies, and whale distribution in relation to oil industry activities.

SCIENTIFIC STYLE

This compilation of research papers and reports focuses on various topics related to marine mammals, with a specific emphasis on dolphins and whales. The document provides information on the anatomy and physiology of their auditory system, their echolocation abilities, sound production and reception, target detection and discrimination, and the use of echolocation for navigation and communication. It also discusses the sensory capabilities, diving behavior, reproductive biology, and other physiological adaptations of marine mammals. Techniques and methods used in the study and management of these animals are described as well. Furthermore, the document includes information on the distribution, abundance, migration patterns, general behavior, and sound production of bowhead whales and gray whales. Additionally, it covers topics such as feeding patterns and habitat preferences of bowhead whales, the selection of marine mammal trainers, capture and adaptation of beluga whales, cytogenetic studies of porpoises, and the distribution of whales relative to oil industry activities. This comprehensive compilation provides valuable insights into the biology, behavior, health, and conservation considerations for marine mammals.

ACTION ITEMS

Read and analyze the research papers and reports to gain a comprehensive understanding of the topics related to marine mammals, particularly dolphins and whales.

Take notes on key findings, methodologies, and conclusions from each paper or report.

Identify any knowledge gaps or areas that require further research.

Consider how the information can be applied to conservation efforts and management strategies for marine mammal populations.

Share relevant findings with colleagues or stakeholders involved in marine mammal research or conservation.

Use the information to inform decision-making processes related to marine mammal protection, habitat preservation, and noise mitigation measures.

Consider potential collaborations

Visual Abstracts

Moods

Figure 1. Marine mammals.

The AI-generated prompt was: Create a black and white illustration that captures the mysterious and majestic nature of marine mammals. Depict a pod of dolphins gracefully swimming through turbulent waters, their sleek bodies cutting through the waves with ease. Show the viewer the power and agility of these creatures as they navigate their watery domain. Capture the emotions of wonder and fascination as each dolphin emits sonar waves, creating ripples in the surrounding water. Let the image convey the intricacies of their auditory system, with abstract lines representing sound waves echoing through the depths. In the distance, illustrate a massive humpback whale breaching, its immense size contrasting against the smaller dolphins. Emphasize its grandeur and strength as it leaps out of the water, creating a sense of awe and admiration for these gentle giants. Through your artwork, transport readers into the world of marine mammals, evoking feelings of intrigue, curiosity, and reverence for these extraordinary creatures.

VIEWPOINTS

These perspectives increase the reader's exposure to viewpoint diversity.

GROUNDS FOR DISSENT

While this document provides a comprehensive overview of various topics related to marine mammals, there may be principled, substantive reasons for a member of the organization responsible for this document to dissent from its findings.

Ethical concerns: One possible reason for dissent could be rooted in ethical considerations regarding the treatment and captivity of marine mammals. The document mentions the selection of marine mammal trainers and the capture and adaptation of beluga whales. A dissenting member might argue that these practices are inherently cruel and inhumane, regardless of any potential scientific knowledge gained from studying captive animals.

Conservation priorities: Another reason for dissent could stem from differing conservation priorities. While the document covers various aspects of marine mammal biology and behavior, it may not address pressing conservation issues adequately. For instance, if a member strongly believes that habitat destruction due to human activities poses a more immediate threat to marine mammals than their auditory system or reproductive biology, they might find the report lacking in addressing these critical concerns.

Methodological criticisms: Dissent may also arise from methodological concerns about the research presented in the document. A member might question the validity or reliability of certain studies included, potentially challenging the overall conclusions drawn from them. This dissent could be driven by a belief that flawed methodology undermines the credibility and applicability of the entire body of research presented.

Omissions and biases: Additionally, a dissenting view might arise due to perceived omissions or biases within the document's content selection. If certain research papers or reports were excluded without proper justification, a member might argue that important perspectives or findings have been disregarded, leading to an incomplete or skewed understanding of marine mammals.

Industry influence: Lastly, a principled reason for dissent could be concerns over industry influence on the document's content. The inclusion of information on whale distribution relative to oil industry activities raises questions about potential conflicts of interest or biased representation. A dissenting member might argue that the document fails to adequately address the negative impacts of human activities on marine mammal populations and instead prioritizes industry concerns.

In summary, a member of the organization responsible for this document may have principled, substantive reasons to dissent based on ethical concerns, differing conservation priorities, methodological criticisms, perceived omissions or biases, or concerns about industry influence. These dissenting views highlight the importance of diverse perspectives in shaping scientific understanding and decision-making processes.

RED TEAM CRITIQUE

The document provides a comprehensive overview of various topics related to marine mammals, specifically dolphins and whales. It covers a wide range of subjects such as anatomy, physiology, echolocation abilities, sound production and reception, target detection and discrimination, as well as the use of echolocation for navigation and communication. The inclusion of these topics suggests that the document aims to offer an in-depth understanding of the auditory system and sensory capabilities of marine mammals.

Furthermore, the document delves into diving behavior, reproductive biology, and other physiological adaptations specific to marine mammals. This provides valuable insights into their biology and behavior which is crucial for studying their health and effective management strategies. The coverage of techniques used in their study adds practical knowledge for researchers working in this field.

The inclusion of information on distribution, abundance, migration patterns, general behavior, sound production by bowhead whales and gray whales is particularly useful for those interested in these species. The discussion on feeding patterns and habitat preferences specific to bowhead whales allows readers to gain a better understanding of their ecological requirements. This can aid conservation efforts by providing information necessary for protected area designation or mitigation measures against potential threats.

Organization: The document lacks a clear organizational structure which makes it difficult for readers to navigate through different sections efficiently. A more organized approach would allow the reader to easily locate specific information without having to search through multiple pages or chapters.

Content: While the document adequately covers a wide range of topics related to marine mammals, there seems to be an imbalance in the depth of coverage for different subject areas. For example, the inclusion of miscellaneous topics such as the selection of marine mammal trainers or cytogenetic studies on porpoises might not be directly relevant to the core focus of this document. It would be more beneficial for readers if these sections were either expanded upon and integrated into the overall narrative or removed altogether.

In conclusion, while this document provides a comprehensive compilation of research papers and reports on various topics related to marine mammals with a focus on dolphins and whales, there are areas that require improvement. A clearer organizational structure with proper citations throughout would enhance its usability and credibility. Additionally, a more focused approach with an emphasis on core subjects directly relevant to the study and management of marine mammals would improve its overall cohesiveness. Overall however high value can still be seen from this compilation as it provides valuable insights into the biology, behavior, health, and management techniques associated with these animals.

MAGA Perspective

This document is yet another example of the liberal agenda trying to distract us from the real issues facing our country. Instead of focusing on the important topics that matter to hardworking Americans, like jobs and the economy, they want us to waste our time reading about dolphins and whales. These creatures have nothing to do with making America great again.

Furthermore, this so-called research is just another way for scientists to push their global warming propaganda. We all know that climate change is a hoax created by the left to control our lives and destroy industries like oil. Studying marine mammals and their behavior is just a part of their plan to convince us that humans are responsible for any changes in their habitat.

Why should we care about the reproductive biology or physiological adaptations of these animals? We have more pressing concerns, such as securing our borders and protecting American jobs. This document is a perfect example of how out-of-touch liberals prioritize the needs of animals over the needs of our own citizens.

Additionally, discussing the selection of marine mammal trainers and the adaptation of beluga whales only serves to promote animal rights extremism. These activists would rather focus on the well-being of animals than on improving the lives of everyday Americans. It's clear where their priorities lie, and it's not with making America great.

In conclusion, this document is just another attempt by the liberal elite to distract us from the issues that truly matter. As patriotic Americans, we must reject this propaganda and stay focused on what really counts: putting America first and making our country prosperous once again.

PAGE-BY-PAGE SUMMARIES

BODY-3 An annotated bibliography of publications from the U.S. Navy's Marine Mammal Program, updated in November 1987.

BODY-5 This page is an annotated bibliography of publications from the U.S. Navy's Marine Mammal Program, including materials from contractors and non-Navy researchers.

BODY-7 This page provides information about the Navy's Marine Mammal Program, including its history and a bibliography of publications by contractors and non-Navy researchers.

BODY-8 The Navy's Marine Mammal Program began in 1960 with the acquisition of a dolphin for hydrodynamic studies. The program evolved into researching marine mammals' senses and abilities, including using trained dolphins for tasks. The program was later incorporated into the Naval Undersea Center and then the Naval Ocean Systems Center.

BODY-9 The page contains a table of contents for a document that covers various topics related to sonar communication, physiology, health care, breeding, behavior, open sea release, tagging and telemetry surveys, hydrodynamics, and miscellaneous subjects.

BODY-10 This page discusses research on cetacean echolocation signals and their potential application to human speech. It also explores the use of dolphin whistles for sonar navigation and Doppler measurement. The page includes measurements of echolocation signals in bottlenose dolphins and an analysis of target recognition via echolocation by an Atlantic bottlenose porpoise.

BODY-11 The page discusses various studies on the echolocation abilities of Atlantic bottlenose dolphins, including their propagation characteristics, target recognition and discrimination behavior, and long-range target detection in open waters.

BODY-12 Various studies on the acoustic behavior and abilities of dolphins, including their echolocation signals, directional hearing, and sonar discrimination capabilities.

BODY-13 The page discusses various studies on echolocation in marine animals, including beluga whales and bottlenose dolphins. It explores how these animals adapt their signals to different environments and examines the neural response to different types of sounds.

BODY-14 The page discusses various studies on the auditory system and echolocation abilities of dolphins, including their responses to different types of sounds and the development of monitoring systems for studying dolphin echolocation.

BODY-15 This page discusses various studies on the underwater sounds produced by gray whales, right whales, and blue whales. It includes findings on the frequency, duration, and intensity of these sounds, as well as their impact on whale behavior.

BODY-16 The page provides information on various studies related to the sound production and behavior of marine mammals, specifically southern right whales and dolphins. It includes details on the types of sounds produced, recording techniques, and discrimination abilities of dolphins using echolocation.

BODY-17 This page discusses various studies on marine mammal communication, including sound production and echolocation. It concludes that while many sounds have social significance, there is no evidence of porpoises possessing a language comparable to humans.

BODY-18 Acoustic source levels of small whales were measured at sea. Models of cetacean signal processing were reviewed, with suggestions for future experiments. Acoustic *noise around Kahoolawe Island was measured during gunnery exercises, and humpback whale behavior was observed. Instrumentation for recording underwater sounds and analyses of cetacean sounds were discussed. The anatomy of the bottlenosed dolphin nasolaryngeal system was described. Auditory thresholds of a killer whale were obtained using operant conditioning techniques*

BODY-19 *The page discusses various studies on target recognition and auditory thresholds in dolphins, including their ability to recognize different target characteristics through echolocation and their sensitivity to different frequencies.*

BODY-20 *The page discusses various studies on the auditory abilities of bottlenose dolphins, including their hearing thresholds, masking curves, and limitations due to thermal noise. It also includes information on dolphin echolocation capacities and the use of microprocessors in collecting and analyzing echolocation data.*

BODY-21 *The page discusses various studies on the communication and sounds of dolphins and whales, including range ambiguity in bottlenose dolphins, communication between dolphins through acoustic links, and recordings of different types of sounds produced by bowhead whales.*

BODY-22 *Human subjects were tested on their ability to discriminate target echoes in white noise using broadband sonar pulses. The experiments showed that humans performed better than dolphins with altered echoes and different signal-to-noise ratios. Additionally, research was conducted on the mechanisms of sound conduction in dolphin ears and the underwater localization abilities of California sea lions.*

BODY-23 *This page contains a list of scientific studies on dolphin echolocation, including experiments on hearing sensitivity, masked thresholds, critical ratios, and target detection performance.*

BODY-24 *The page contains abstracts and reviews of various studies on the echolocation abilities of dolphins, including their performance on different reinforcement schedules, discrimination of object size and shape, and sensory modality transfer. It also includes a reference to 20-Hz signals observed in the Central Pacific, potentially from finback whales.*

BODY-25 *Various studies on underwater signals and echolocation abilities of different species of dolphins and porpoises.*

BODY-26 *The page discusses various studies on the sound production and hearing abilities of dolphins and sea lions, including anatomical and physiological findings, proposed methods for field studies, and correlations between sound production and behavior.*

BODY-27 *Varying the payoff matrix can control response bias in experiments with marine mammals detecting underwater signals. Echolocation studies of marine mammals require comprehensive methodology and experimental design. Response bias strongly influences attention in discriminative echolocation tasks for dolphins. Northern fur seals and California sea lions are more sensitive to airborne sounds than other pinnipeds. Training dolphins to emit echolocation pulses on cue solves the problem of ambiguous echo returns. A bottlenose porpoise can detect a target using listening instead of ech*

BODY-28 *Studies on gray seals and other marine mammals' echolocation capabilities, underwater recordings of pinniped sounds, and long-term monitoring of whale sounds off Oahu are discussed.*

BODY-29 *No significant difference in target detection performance between beluga whales and bottlenose dolphins at various distances. Descriptions of the ambient noise in the ocean and the cochlea structure of dolphins, suggesting their high auditory proficiency and ability to utilize auditory information.*

BODY-30   The page discusses the adaptiveness and ecology of echolocation in toothed whales, focusing on the relationship between echolocation signal characteristics and ecological niches. It suggests that certain asymmetrical features and differences in brain size are related to the development and versatility of their sonar system.

BODY-31   This page contains summaries of various studies on dolphins, including their muscle characteristics, skin thickness, chemical communication, respiratory water exchange, and eye movements.

BODY-32   This page contains references to various scientific studies on the anatomy and physiology of marine mammals, including dolphins and whales. The studies cover topics such as ocular fundus photography, corneal surface properties, telemetering of temperature and depth data, neuroanatomy of the spinal cord, and physiological parameters of blood.

BODY-33   This page contains a list of scientific articles discussing various aspects of blood values, electrocardiograms, gonadal activity, telemetry, and diving in seals and dolphins.

BODY-34   Porpoises and sea lions with faster swimming and longer dives have greater hemoglobin oxygen affinity. Thoracic collapse in dolphins reduces displacement stress on abdominal organs during diving. Dentin layers in teeth can be used for age determination in Tursiops truncatus. Correlation between various factors and sexual maturity in common dolphins was determined statistically. Captive dolphins have low total body water, indicating high water turnover due to skin permeability. Cetaceans have evolved physiological adaptations for deep diving and nutrient movement

BODY-35   This page provides a list of research articles on various topics related to marine mammals, including their reproductive status, food habits, chemoreception, renal function, and sensory capabilities.

BODY-36   This page discusses various research studies conducted on dolphins and porpoises, including their visual acuity, blood oxygen content, diving abilities, hematologic findings, thyroid function, and buoyancy regulation.

BODY-37   This page discusses various research studies conducted on diving physiology, hearing, sleep, and brain temperatures in dolphins, sea lions, and seals. It includes information on anesthesia procedures, surgical techniques for measuring cochlear electrophysiology, conditioned bradycardia in sea lions, sleep patterns in gray seals, auditory-evoked potentials in seals, and brain size asymmetry in dolphin genera.

BODY-38   The page discusses various studies on dolphins, including their lung collapse during diving, auditory brainstem responses, weight-length relationships, diving capabilities, brain sizes, and diving hazards.

BODY-39   This page discusses various topics related to cetaceans, including brain size, diving capabilities, physiological observations on dolphin brains, and techniques for studying biophysical data and hearing in marine mammals.

BODY-40   A comparison of the microscopic anatomy of marine mammals, a radiographic atlas of the California sea lion, and research on auditory event-related potentials in dolphins.

BODY-41   Various studies on the health, nutrition, and pathology of dolphins, including antibiotic levels, cranial abscesses, nutrition, stomatitis, antibody levels, cerebral abscesses, and transportation-associated myopathy.

BODY-42   Dolphin lymphocytes respond to certain substances, which could enhance their immune response. A new species of parasitic flatworm is described. A fluke found in a dolphin's ear could impair hearing. Premature births in sea lions are associated with high levels of pollutants. Fatal bronchopneumonia and edema disease are identified in dolphins and sea lions. Vaccination of porpoises against infection is discussed.

BODY-43 The page discusses various studies on marine mammals, including premature parturition in California sea lions, the presence of Salmonella in fur seals and sea lions, survivorship patterns in captive killer whales, parasitism in marine mammals, mercury-selenium-bromine imbalance in sea lions, a clinical temperature telemetry system for sea lions, and the effects of prolonged halothane anesthesia on cetaceans.

BODY-44 The page provides a collection of articles on various medical aspects related to marine mammals, including diagnosis and treatment of diseases, blood groups in porpoises, anesthesia techniques for sea lions and porpoises, and the use of bottlenose dolphins in biomedical research.

BODY-45 This page discusses various topics related to anesthesia and diseases in marine mammals, including the anesthetization of porpoises, trematode parasites in dolphins, diseases in pinnipeds, tooth extraction in bottlenosed dolphins, and causes of death in captive killer whales.

BODY-46 The page discusses various studies on dolphin hearing, sound production, and health. It also includes reports on infections in dolphins and other marine mammals, as well as the potential transfer of diseases between marine and land animals.

BODY-47 Calicivirus transmitted between dolphins and sea lions, regression of tattoo lesions in dolphins linked to poxvirus, transfusion of heterologous red blood cells in sea lions, diseases and clinical management of pinnipeds and small cetaceans.

BODY-48 The page discusses systemic mycoses in marine mammals, the use of intratracheal injections of antibiotics in sea lions and dolphins, contingency rations for California sea lions, and diets for marine mammals.

BODY-49 This page contains a list of papers on breeding dolphins, including topics such as semen collection, growth patterns, hormone fluctuations, ovulation in captivity, and social behavior of dolphin calves.

BODY-50 The page discusses difficult births, neonatal health problems, and diagnosis of pregnancy in small cetaceans using various techniques. It also includes information on porpoise births at Marineland, Florida and the challenges of captive breeding.

BODY-51 This page discusses various studies on marine mammal behavior and training, including the effects of reinforcement schedules on dolphin behavior, auditory problem-solving abilities of bottlenose dolphins, and spatial habit reversal in marine mammals. It also mentions a study on shape discrimination and problem-solving abilities in dolphins and the behavior of southern right whales.

BODY-52 The page discusses various observations of behavior in small cetaceans, including waking, swimming, and sleeping patterns. It also mentions the use of collateral behaviors in training marine mammals and the feeding behaviors of bottlenose dolphins.

BODY-53 This page provides brief summaries of various studies on the behavior of dolphins and killer whales, including their swimming patterns, diving modes, hunting behaviors, and responses to different types of reinforcement.

BODY-54 This page provides summaries of various research articles on dolphin behavior, including training techniques for trainers, comparisons of sensory capabilities between different types of seals and sea lions, interactions between porpoises and sharks, and social behavior and feeding strategies of dolphins.

BODY-55 This page provides brief descriptions of various projects involving the training and release of marine mammals for object recovery in the open sea.

BODY-56 The page describes the training of a bottlenose porpoise to dive to depths of 550 feet and perform tasks for the Sealab II program. It also discusses the development of a float to prevent sea lions from swimming away during training and the use of a dolphin named Tuffy to carry objects between the surface and aquanauts.

BODY-57 This page discusses various studies and techniques used to track and study the behavior of whales and dolphins, including the use of telemetry and tagging methods. It also mentions how underwater topography and prey availability can influence the distribution patterns of dolphins.

BODY-58 The page discusses various techniques and surveys conducted to estimate the population of bottlenose dolphins and sea otters in different areas. It also mentions aerial surveys of whales and their behavior in the Beaufort Sea, Chukchi Sea, and northern Bering Sea.

BODY-59 Aerial surveys of endangered whales in the northern Bering, eastern Chukchi, and Alaskan Beaufort Seas from 1979-1985. Includes observations on bowhead and gray whale distribution, abundance, migration patterns, behavior, and feeding patterns.

BODY-60 This page contains references to various studies on the distribution, abundance, behavior, and sound production of endangered whales in the Alaskan Beaufort and eastern Chukchi Seas. The studies also include observations on gray whale distribution and other marine mammal sightings.

BODY-61 The page discusses the summer distribution of bowhead whales in relation to oil industry activities in the Canadian Beaufort Sea. It mentions that the distribution varied from year to year and that the number of whales decreased, but it is unclear whether this was due to industrial activity or changes in their prey. Another section describes a surgical technique used to attach a telemetry device to a California gray whale.

BODY-62 Various studies on the hydrodynamic characteristics of dolphins, including swimming speeds and performance tests, show that their energy expenditure is within expected ranges and no extraordinary mechanisms are needed to explain their observations. The reported speeds of cetaceans and fish can be explained by an unusual extent of laminar flow.

BODY-63 Dolphin fin profiles have a unique shape that combines two hydrodynamic shapes, potentially giving them superior characteristics. Dolphin skin properties were also measured using acoustic surface waves.

BODY-64 This page contains summaries of various research studies on marine mammal trainers, beluga whales, porpoises, dolphins, pilot whales, and blind river dolphins. The studies cover topics such as selection procedures for trainers, capture and adaptation techniques for belugas, cytogenetic studies of porpoises, hematologic differences in dolphins, stranding investigations of pilot whales, and behavior observations of blind river dolphins.

BODY-65 The page discusses various topics related to cetaceans, including their distributions, chromosomes, identification, and acoustic target strengths. It also mentions the observation of a gray whale calf being born outside of its normal calving area.

BODY-66 The page discusses brain-spinal cord ratios in porpoises as a possible indicator of intelligence. It also includes information on the natural history and captivity of Dall's porpoises, as well as references to handbooks on marine mammals and studies on sea lion homing behavior.

BODY-67 This page provides information on two books written by F.G. Wood. The first book discusses the Navy's marine mammal program and porpoises, while the second book explores the phenomenon of cetacean strandings and proposes a hypothesis for their cause.

NOTABLE PASSAGES

BODY-8   *"Primary interest was in marine mammals - the study of their specially developed senses and systems, such as sonar and deep-diving physiology - and also how porpoises and sea lions might be used to perform useful tasks."*

BODY-15   *"Powerful, three-part sounds lasting about 36.5 seconds and ranging in frequency from 12.5 to 200 Hz were recorded from blue whales off the coast of Chile. Their 'moanings,' estimated to be 188 dB re 1 u N/m2 = (=88 dB re 1 /pbar) at 1 meter, are the most powerful sustained utterances known from whales or any other living source."*

BODY-26   *"Study of the gross and microanatomical nature of the nasal plug nodes, diagonal membrane, and nasofrontal sacs, coupled with acoustic, electromyographic. and pressure measurements strongly indicated that this system constitutes the source of sound production."*

BODY-34   *"Porpoises which swim faster and dive longer and deeper have greater hemoglobin oxygen affinity than the slower-swimming, shallower and shorter-diving species."*

BODY-43   *"The data suggested a very strong relationship between Hg, Se, and Br in the normal animals but a Br imbalance, in relation to Se and Hg, in the abnormal mothers and their pups."*

BODY-49   *"Robustness Quotient" appears to provide a good indicator for female sexual maturity, while a "Flipper Index" (derived from radiographs showing a degree of epiphyseal fusion) provides an estimate of gonad development in males.*

BODY-52   *"Observed behavior consisted of periods of unambiguous waking, stereotypic circular swimming with brief (20-30 sec) eye closure and other indications of sleep. and quiescent 'hanging' behavior with similar indications of sleep."*

BODY-56   *"Total dive time to 550 feet and back averaged 163 seconds."*

BODY-66   *"It has been suggested that brain weight:spinal cord weight ratios may provide a rough index of intelligence in vertebrate animals. This ratio in the bottlenose porpoise average 40:1, as compared to the 50:1 ratio in man."*

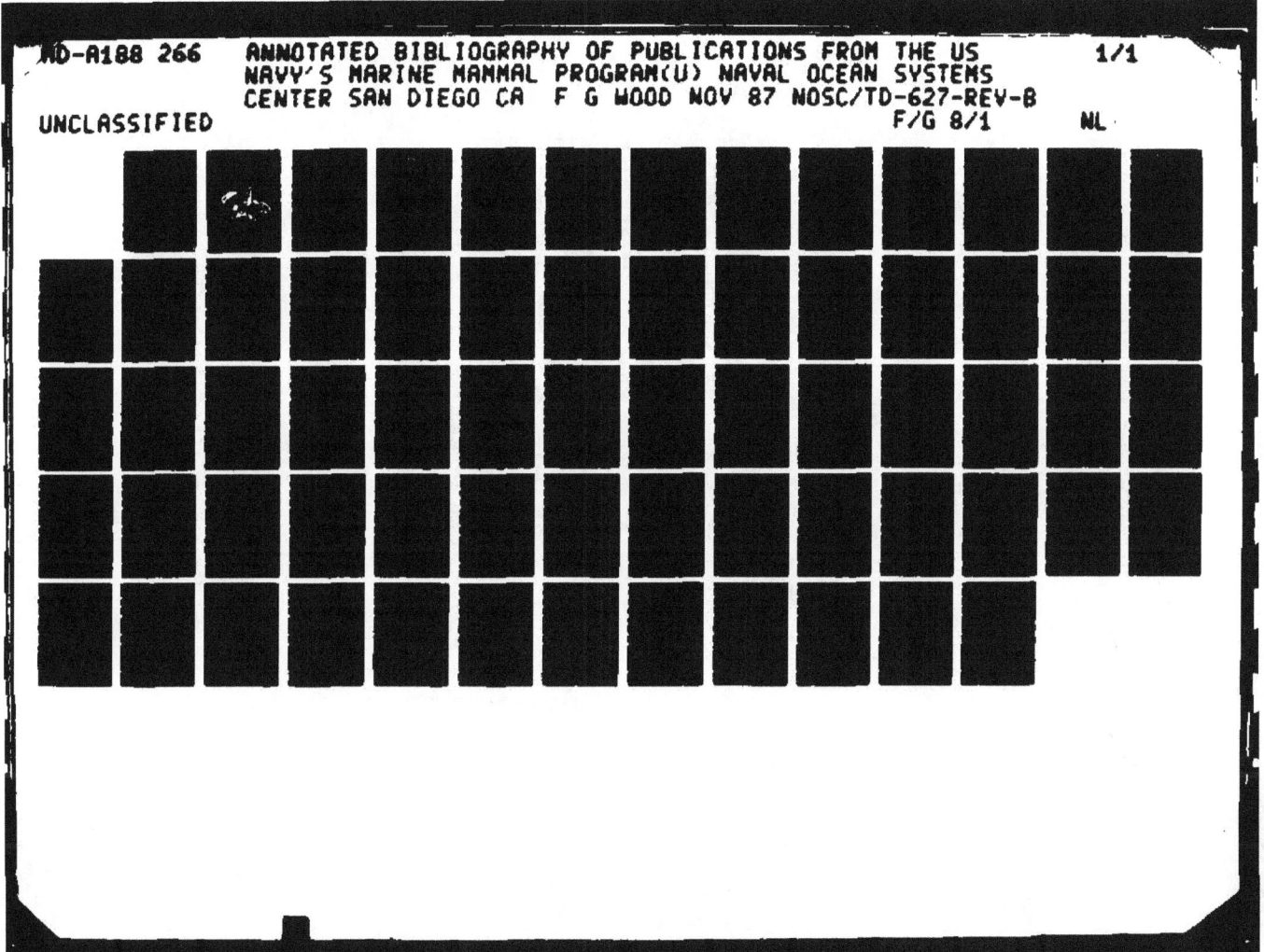

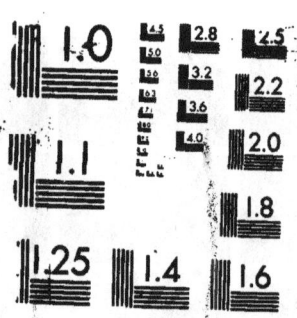

NOSC Technical Document 627
Revision B

DTIC FILE COPY

Annotated Bibliography of Publications from the U.S. Navy's Marine Mammal Program

UPDATE
November 1987

Approved for public release; distribution is unlimited.

**NAVAL OCEAN SYSTEMS CENTER
SAN DIEGO, CA 92152-5000**

NAVAL OCEAN SYSTEMS CENTER
San Diego, California 92152-5000

E. G. SCHWEIZER, CAPT, USN
Commander

R. M. HILLYER
Technical Director

ADMINISTRATIVE INFORMATION

This bibliography was compiled and updated by Forrest G. Wood, Code 514, Naval Ocean Systems Center, San Diego, California 92152-5000.

Special acknowledgement to Hans-es-Biene Abt for providing the cover design.

Released by
L.W. Bivens, Head
Biological Sciences
Branch

Under authority of
H.O. Porter, Head
Biosciences Division

MA

UNCLASSIFIED
SECURITY CLASSIFICATION OF THIS PAGE

AD-A188 266

REPORT DOCUMENTATION PAGE

1a. REPORT SECURITY CLASSIFICATION UNCLASSIFIED	1b. RESTRICTIVE MARKINGS			
2a. SECURITY CLASSIFICATION AUTHORITY	3. DISTRIBUTION/AVAILABILITY OF REPORT			
2b. DECLASSIFICATION/DOWNGRADING SCHEDULE	Approved for public release; distribution is unlimited.			
4. PERFORMING ORGANIZATION REPORT NUMBER(S) NOSC TD 627 Revision B	5. MONITORING ORGANIZATION REPORT NUMBER(S)			
6a. NAME OF PERFORMING ORGANIZATION Naval Ocean Systems Center	6b. OFFICE SYMBOL (If applicable) Code 514	7a. NAME OF MONITORING ORGANIZATION		
6c. ADDRESS (City, State and ZIP Code) San Diego, CA 92152-5000	7b. ADDRESS (City, State and ZIP Code)			
8a. NAME OF FUNDING/SPONSORING ORGANIZATION Naval Sea Systems Command	8b. OFFICE SYMBOL (If applicable) NSEA-06G6	9. PROCUREMENT INSTRUMENT IDENTIFICATION NUMBER		
8c. ADDRESS (City, State and ZIP Code) Washington, DC 20362-5101	10. SOURCE OF FUNDING NUMBERS			
	PROGRAM ELEMENT NO 63709N	PROJECT NO SO214	TASK NO 510-MM40	AGENCY ACCESSION NO DN788 737

11. TITLE (Include Security Classification)
Annotated Bibliography of Publications from the U.S. Navy's Marine Mammal Program

12. PERSONAL AUTHOR(S)
F.G. Wood

13a. TYPE OF REPORT Bibliography	13b. TIME COVERED FROM ___ TO ___	14. DATE OF REPORT (Year, Month, Day) November 1987	15. PAGE COUNT 66

16. SUPPLEMENTARY NOTATION

17. COSATI CODES			18. SUBJECT TERMS (Continue on reverse if necessary and identify by block number)
FIELD	GROUP	SUB-GROUP	

19. ABSTRACT (Continue on reverse if necessary and identify by block number)

The Navy's Marine Mammal Program is conducted by the Naval Ocean Systems Center, San Diego, California. Entries in this bibliography include publications by contractors and by other non-Navy researchers whose materials or facilities were provided by the Navy.

20. DISTRIBUTION/AVAILABILITY OF ABSTRACT ☐ UNCLASSIFIED/UNLIMITED ☒ SAME AS RPT ☐ DTIC USERS	21. ABSTRACT SECURITY CLASSIFICATION UNCLASSIFIED	
22a. NAME OF RESPONSIBLE INDIVIDUAL F. G. Wood	22b. TELEPHONE (Include Area Code) (619) 553-7621	22c. OFFICE SYMBOL Code 514

DD FORM 1473, 84 JAN 83 APR EDITION MAY BE USED UNTIL EXHAUSTED
ALL OTHER EDITIONS ARE OBSOLETE

UNCLASSIFIED
SECURITY CLASSIFICATION OF THIS PAGE

UNCLASSIFIED
SECURITY CLASSIFICATION OF THIS PAGE (When Data Entered)

DD FORM 1473, 84 JAN

UNCLASSIFIED
SECURITY CLASSIFICATION OF THIS PAGE (When Data Entered)

FOREWORD

The Navy's Marine Mammal Program, originally a cooperative effort of the Naval Ordnance Test Station and the Naval Missile Center, is now conducted by the Naval Ocean Systems Center, at San Diego, California, and Kaneohe Bay, Hawaii. For a brief history of the program see p. ii.

Entries in this bibliography include publications by contractors and by other non-Navy researchers whose materials or facilities were provided by the Navy.

In-house publications are identified by the acronyms NOTS (Naval Ordnance Test Station), NUC (Naval Undersea Center), NSWC (Naval Surface Weapons Center), and NOSC (Naval Ocean Systems Center). These publications consist of TPs (Technical Publications), TRs (Technical Reports), and TDs (Technical Documents).

The majority of the papers listed were published in established technical journals or books which are available at libraries or through interlibrary loan. Copies of the in-house publications can be obtained from the National Technical Information Service, Springfield, VA 22161; the cost varies according to the size of the document.

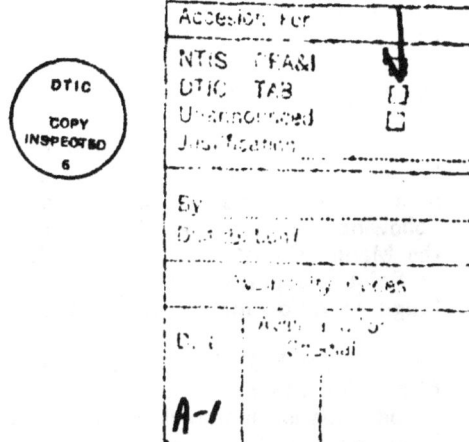

BRIEF HISTORY OF THE NAVY'S MARINE MAMMAL PROGRAM

The Navy's Marine Mammal Program had its origin in the acquisition, in 1960, of a Pacific white-sided dolphin for hydrodynamic studies. Scientists of the Naval Ordnance Test Station (NOTS) at China Lake and Pasadena, California, had heard accounts of the hydrodynamic efficiency of porpoises. Since NOTS was in the business of (among other things) designing and developing torpedoes, it seemed reasonable to find out whether porpoises did in fact have special characteristics that might be applied to the design of the underwater missiles.

Work with the white-sided dolphin, named Notty, revealed no unusual physiological or hydrodynamic capabilities, but it was suspected that conditions in the long testing tank in which she swam might have affected her performance. The NOTS scientists and engineers wanted to continue their investigation of porpoises, and looked about for an appropriate site at which to establish a small research facility.

They found such a site at Point Mugu, California, where the Pacific Missile Range and Naval Missile Center were located. By coincidence, a group in the Life Sciences Department of the Naval Missile Center was also proposing to undertake studies of marine life, including porpoises. Mugu Lagoon, the last such body of protected water on the Southern California coast, was seen as a great asset for such work.

As a result of these mutual interests, and with encouragement from the Office of Naval Research, a modest facility for research and exploratory development gradually evolved on a sand spit between the lagoon and the ocean at Point Mugu. The program got underway in 1963. Primary interest was in marine mammals - the study of their specially developed senses and systems, such as sonar and deep-diving physiology - and also how porpoises and sea lions might be used to perform useful tasks. A major accomplishment was the demonstration that trained porpoises and sea lions could be worked untethered in the open sea with great reliability. In 1965, a Navy bottlenose dolphin named Tuffy participated in the Sea Lab II project off La Jolla, California, carrying tools and messages between the surface and aquanauts operating out of the habitat 200 feet below.

In 1967, the Point Mugu facility and its personnel, both of NOTS and the Naval Missile Center, were placed under a newly formed organization which was to become the Naval Undersea Center (NUC), with headquarters in San Diego. Following the formation of the Center, a NUC laboratory was established in Hawaii at the Marine Corps Air Station on Kaneohe Bay. Some of the personnel and animals at Point Mugu transferred to the Hawaii laboratory, and later the rest of the Point Mugu operation moved to San Diego.

In March 1977, the Naval Undersea Center was combined with the nearby Naval Electronics Laboratory Center to form the Naval Ocean Systems Center (NOSC). The ongoing marine mammal research and development work of the San Diego and Hawaii laboratories continues as an important part of NOSC's total effort.

CONTENTS:

		Page
1.	SOUND/SONAR/COMMUNICATION	1
2.	PHYSIOLOGY/ANATOMY/GROWTH AND AGING	23
3.	HEALTH CARE/NUTRITION/PATHOLOGY	33
4.	BREEDING	41
5.	BEHAVIOR/PSYCHOPHYSICS	43
6.	OPEN SEA RELEASE	47
7.	TAGGING/TELEMETRY/SURVEYS	49
8.	HYDRODYNAMICS	55
9.	MISCELLANEOUS	57

1. SOUND/SONAR/COMMUNICATION

Altes, R. A., W. E. Evans, C. S. Johnson 1975 Cetacean echolocation signals and a new model for the human glottal pulse. Jour. Acoust. Soc. Am. *57*(5):1221-1224.

A theoretical explanation for cetacean sonar systems can also be applied to human speech. The theory leads to a mathematical model of the human glottal pulse that is considerably different from those employed in the past.

Altes, Richard and S. H. Ridgway 1980 Dolphin whistles as velocity-sensitive sonar/navigation signals. In: *Animal Sonar Systems*, pp. 853-854 (ed. R.-G. Busnel and J.F. Fish), Plenum Press.

A certain type of dolphin whistle which has been classified as a distress whistle but which also occurs under other circumstances is very similar to signals that can be used for accurate Doppler measurement. On theoretical grounds, such whistles have characteristics that might make them useful for sonar navigation, but behavioral experiments are needed.

Au, W. W. L. 1980 Echolocation signals of the Atlantic bottlenose dolphin (*Tursiops truncatus*) in open waters. In: *Animal Sonar Systems*, pp. 251-282 (ed. R.-G. Busnel and J. F. Fish), Plenum Press.

A review, with additional previously unpublished data.

Au, W. W. L., R. W. Floyd, R. H. Penner and A. E. Murchison 1974 Measurement of echolocation signals in the Atlantic bottlenose dolphin, *Tursiops truncatus* Montagu, in open waters. Jour. Acoust. Soc. Am. *56*(4)1280-1290.

Echolocation signals of two bottlenose dolphins echolocating on targets at distances of 60 to 80 yards were measured. Peak energies between 120 and 130 kHz, were recorded, with sound pressure levels at least 30 dB higher than any previously reported.

Au, W. W. L., and Clifford Hammer 1978 Analysis of target recognition via echolocation by an Atlantic bottlenose porpoise (*Tursiops truncatus*). (Abstract) Jour. Acoust. Soc. Am. Vol. 64, Suppl. 1, p. S87.

From targets previously used for a study of porpoise echolocation, echoes of porpoise-like signals were obtained and analyzed. The shape of the spectrum was predominantly influenced by the first two echo components, those from the front face and the interior boundary of the rear face. Matched-filter analysis corresponds closely with the animal's performance.

Au, W. W. L., R. W. Floyd and J. E. Haun 1978 Propagation of Atlantic bottlenose dolphin echolocation signals. Jour. Acoust. Soc. Am. 64:411-422.

The propagational characteristics of high-frequency signals (peak energies above 100 kHz) were determined by a series of measurements made in open water. The 3-dB broadband beamwidth was found to be approximately 10" in both the horizontal and vertical planes. The major axis of the vertical beam was directed at an angle of 20" above the plane defined by the animal's teeth.

Au, W. W. L., and C. E. Hammer 1980 Target recognition via echolocation by *Tursiops truncatus*. In: *Animal Sonar Systems*, pp. 855-858 (ed. R.-G. Busnel and J. F. Fish), Plenum Press.

Target recognition and discrimination behavior was studied as a function of target composition and internal structure. The targets were then acoustically examined using a simulated dolphin echolocation signal in order to determine the salient cues that could enable the animal to discriminate the targets.

Au, W. W. L., R. J. Schusterman and D. A. Kersting 1980 Sphere-cylinder discrimination via echolocation by *Tursiops truncatus*. In: *Animal Sonar Systems*, pp. 859-862 (ed. R.-G. Busnel and J. F. Fish), Plenum Press.

Discrimination of spherical and cylindrical targets of the same material but in dimensions such that they had overlapping target strengths was demonstrated. Acoustic examination of echoes from the targets indicated that they were very similar, but it was found that the water-surface-reflected component of the echoes differed with the two shapes and apparently provided the essential cue.

Au, W. W. L. and K. J. Snyder 1980 Long-range target detection in open waters by an echolocating Atlantic bottlenose dolphin. Jour. Acoust. Soc. Am. 68(4):1077-1084.

The dolphin was found to be capable of detecting a 7.62-cm diameter stainless steel water-filled sphere at 113 m (50% target detection threshold range). Results with this sphere were congruent with those obtained previously with a sphere of less than half its diameter.

Au, W. W. L. and R. H. Penner 1981 Target detection in noise by echolocating Atlantic bottlenose dolphins. Jour. Acoust. Soc. Am. 70(3):687-693.

The capability of two dolphins to detect a 7.62-cm water-filled stainless steel sphere was tested in the presence of white noise. The response of an ideal energy detector was found to match the behavioral results as a function of the echo signal-to-noise ratio.

2

Au, W. W. L., R. H. Penner and James Kadane 1982 Acoustic behavior of echolocating Atlantic bottlenose dolphins. Jour. Acoust. Soc. Am. 71(5):1269-1275.

A click detector was used to monitor acoustic emissions of two dolphins performing a target detection task in white noise. Average number of clicks emitted per trial increased with masking noise until a particular level was reached, then decreased with further increases in noise level. Response levels and click intervals were also analyzed.

Au, W. W. L. and P. W. B. Moore 1982 Directional hearing in the Atlantic bottlenose dolphin *Tursiops truncatus*. (Abstract) Jour. Acoust. Soc. Am. Vol. 70, Suppl. 1, p. S42.

Directional hearing sensitivity in the horizontal plane was measured for pure-tone frequencies of 30, 60, and 120 kHz (for vertical beam pattern results see Moore & Au 1981). The receiving directivity index for beam patterns in both the vertical and horizontal planes was 10, 15, and 21 dB respectively for the three frequencies.

Au, W. W. L. D. A. Carter, R. H. Penner, and B.L. Scronce 1982 Beluga whale echolocation signals in two different ambient noise environments. Jour. Acoust. Soc. Am. Vol. 72, Suppl. 1, p. S42.

In Kaneohe Bay, Hawaii, the echolocation clicks emitted by a beluga during a target identification task had higher peak frequencies and higher bandwidths than were measured earlier in the lower ambient noise environment of San Diego Bay.

Au, W. W. L., and D. W. Martin 1983 Insights into dolphin sonar discrimination capabilities from broadband sonar discrimination experiments with human subjects. (Abstract) Jour. Acoust. Soc. Am. Vol. 74, Suppl. 1, p. S73.

When digital recordings made of echoes from targets ensonified with a dolphin-like signal were played back at a slower rate to subjects, humans could make fine target discriminations about as well as dolphins can under less controlled conditions.

Au, W. W. L., and P. W. B. Moore 1984 Receiving beam patterns and directivity indices of the Atlantic bottlenose dolphin *Tursiops truncatus*. Jour. Acoust. Soc. Am. 75(1):255-262.

Receiving beam patterns were measured in both the vertical and horizontal planes for frequencies of 30, 60, and 120 kHz. Beam patterns in both planes became narrower as the frequency increased.

Au, W. W. L., and C. W. Turl 1984 Dolphin biosonar detection in clutter: Variation in the payoff matrix. Jour. Acoust. Soc. Am. 76(3):955-957.

A bottlenose dolphin was trained to detect targets in the interference of a clutter screen (spaced cork spheres in a rectangular array). The number of pieces of fish given for correct detections and rejections was varied. Increased food reinforcement resulted in an increase in both correct detection and false alarm rates, but detection sensitivity was approximately constant.

Au, W. W. L., D. A. Carder, R. H. Penner, and B. L. Scronce 1985 Demonstration of adaptation in beluga whale echolocation signals. Jour. Acoust. Soc. Am. 77(2):726-730.

The echolocation signals of the same beluga were measured first in San Diego Bay and later in Kaneohe Bay, Hawaii, where the ambient noise level was much higher. In Kaneohe Bay the beluga shifted its signals to higher frequencies and intensities.

Au, W. W. L., P. W. B. Moore, and Deborah Pawloski 1986 Echolocation transmitting beam of the Atlantic bottlenose dolphin. Jour. Acoust. Soc. Am. 80:688-691.

The transmitting beam patterns of echolocation signals were measured in the vertical and horizontal planes with an array of seven hydrophones.

Bastian, J., C. Wall and C. L. Anderson 1966 The transmission of arbitrary environmental information between bottlenose dolphins. In: *Animal Sonar Systems - Biology and Bionics*, Vol. II, pp. 803-873 (ed. R.-G. Busnel) Laboratoire de Physiologieustique, Jouy-en-Josas 78, France.

Bastian, J., C. Wall and C. L. Anderson 1968 Further investigation of the transmission of arbitrary information between bottlenose dolphins. NUWC TP 109, 40 pp.

The above two papers describe studies designed to ascertain if one dolphin could, by acoustic signals, "tell" another, partitioned from the first, to push one or the other of two paddles. After training, the animals performed correctly, but analysis of recordings indicated that they were responding to self-taught cues, with no comprehension of the task.

Bullock, T. H., S. H. Ridgway and Nobua Suga 1971 Acoustically evoked potentials in midbrain auditory structures in sea lions (Pinnipedia). Z. vergl. Physiologie 74:372-387.

Electrophysiological experiments were conducted to determine neural response to different types of sounds. The results could not settle the question as to whether sea lions employ echolocation, but they indicated lack of specialization for the types of sounds bats and porpoises use.

Bullock, T. H., and S. H. Ridgway 1972 Neurophysiological findings relevant to echolocation in marine animals. In: *Animal Orientation and Navigation*, pp. 373-395 (ed. S. R. Galler et al.) National Aeronautics and Space Administration Publication SP-262.

A review.

Bullock, T. H., and S. H. Ridgway 1972 Evoked potentials in the central auditory system of alert porpoises to their own and artificial sounds. Jour. of Neurobiology 3(1):79-99.

Among other findings it was noted that high-intensity clicks often evoked quite modest potentials, while a much weaker click gave maximum potentials. This suggested that differences in click composition are quite important to a porpoise.

Caldwell, M. C., D. K. Caldwell and W. E. Evans 1966 Sounds and behavior of captive Amazon dolphins, *Inia geoffrensis*. Contributions in Science, Los Angeles County Museum, No. 108, 24 pp.

Inia emits pulsed phonations that could be used for echolocation. The freshwater dolphins were not fearful of strange objects (as *Tursiops* usually is) and exhibited curiosity and playfulness.

Carder, D. A., and S. H. Ridgway 1983 Apparent echolocation by a sixty-day-old bottlenose dolphin, *Tursiops truncatus*. (Abstract) Jour. Acoust. Soc. Am. Vol. 74, Suppl. 1, p. S74.

Squeals were heard about 10 sec after birth and whistlelike calls soon after, but high-frequency pulses, with head-scanning movements, were not noticed prior to 60 days.

Ceruti, M. G., P. W. B. Moore, and S. A. Patterson 1983 Peak sound pressure level and spectral frequency distributions in echolocation pulses of Atlantic bottlenose dolphins, *Tursiops truncatus*. (Abstract) Jour. Acoust. Soc. Amer. Vol. 73, Suppl. 1, p. S73.

Peaks in the averaged bimodal pulse spectrum occurred at 60 and 135 kHz or beyond, while the averaged unimodal pulse spectrum peaked at 120 kHz. Abstract includes other findings.

Ceruti, M. G., and W. W. L. Au 1983 Microprocessor-based system for monitoring a dolphin's echolocation pulse parameters. Jour. Acoust. Soc. Am. 73(4):1390-1392.

Describes development of an on-line data acquisition system which includes a device for measuring the frequency spectrum of transient pulses between 30 and 135 kHz and discusses applications of the system in dolphin echolocation experiments.

Cummings, W. C., P. O. Thompson and R. C. Cook 1967 Sound production of migrating gray whales, *Eschrichtius gibbosus* Erxleben. (Abstract) Jour. of Acoust. Soc. Am. 44(5):1211.

Abstract of a paper presented to the ASA which reports low frequency moaning sounds from gray whales while they were migrating to Mexico from the Bering Sea.

Cummings, W. C., P. O. Thompson and R. D. Cooke 1968 Underwater sounds of migrating gray whales, *Eschrichtius glaucus* (Cope). Jour. Acoust. Soc. Am. 44(5)1278-1281.

   Includes methods, results, and discussion of work done on sound production of gray whales. Three categories of sounds range in frequency from 15 to 305 Hz at source levels up to 52 dB re 1 microbar at 1 yd. New findings concerning gray whale behavior are presented.

Cummings, W. C., and L. A. Philippi 1970 Whale Phonations in repetitive stanzas. NUC TP 196, 4 pp.

   Recordings of low frequency sounds from what were probably right whales revealed very similar stanzas lasting 11 to 14 minutes. Stanzas were repeated every 8 to 10 minutes.

Cummings, W. C., and P. O. Thompson 1971 Underwater sounds from the blue whale, *Balaenoptera musculus*. Jour. Acoust. Soc. Am. 50(4, Pt. 2):1193-1198.

   Powerful, three-part sounds lasting about 36.5 seconds and ranging in frequency from 12.5 to 200 Hz were recorded from blue whales off the coast of Chile. Their "moanings," estimated to be 188 dB re 1 u N/m^2 = (=88 dB re 1 μbar) at 1 meter, are the most powerful sustained utterances known from whales or any other living source.

Cummings, W. C., et al. 1971 Bioacoustics of marine animals of Argentina, R/V *Hero* cruise 71-3. Antarctic Jour. of the U.S. 6(6):266-268.

   Describes sounds of cetaceans and pinnipeds recorded along the coast of Argentina.

Cummings, W. C., and J. F. Fish 1971 Bioacoustics of cetaceans. Alpha Helix Research Program, 1971, U. of Calif., San Diego, p. 29.

   Discusses the likelihood that 20-Hz signals are produced by the blue whale.

Cummings, W. C., and P. O. Thompson 1971 Gray whales, *Eschrichtius robustus*, avoid the underwater sounds of killer whales. Fishery Bulletin 69(3):525-530.

   Recorded sounds of killer whales were transmitted underwater to gray whales as the latter were migrating south to Baja California. In most instances the gray whales swam away from the sound source. Pure-tone sounds and random noise had no effect.

Cummings, W. C., and P. O. Thompson 1971 Bioacoustics of marine mammals; R/V *Hero* cruise 70-3. Antarctic Jour. of the U.S. 6(5):158-160.

   Brief account of cruise of the NSF research vessel Hero from Punta Arenas to Valparaiso, Chile. Sounds of blue whales as well as South American fur seals and sea lions were recorded. No underwater vocalizations were detected from Guadalupe fur seals.

Cummings, W. C., J. F. Fish and P. O. Thompson 1972 Sound production and other behavior of southern right whales, *Eubalaena glacialis*. Trans. San Diego Soc. Nat. Hist. *17*(1):1-13.

The underwater sounds were recorded in Golfo San Jose, Argentina, in late June and early July, 1971. The most common was a belch-like utterance with most energy below 500 Hz. The whales also produced two kinds of "moans" and miscellaneous other sounds. Observed behavior suggested bottom feeding.

Diercks, K. J., and W. E. Evans 1969 Delphinid sonar: Pulse wave and simulation studies. NUC TP 175, 84 pp.

A series of reports, primarily by Applied Research Laboratories, U. of Texas, on analysis of the dolphin's emitted signal forms and simple target-echo forms, and a similar consideration of simulated pulses and their echoes. The data are largely preliminary to more detailed analyses.

Diercks, K. J., R. T. Trochta, C. F. Greenlaw and W. E. Evans 1971 Recording and analysis of dolphin echolocation signals. Jour. Acoust. Soc. Am. *49*(6, Pt. 1):1729-1732.

Describes techniques of recording sonar signals by transducers attached by small suction cups to a porpoise's head and body, with examples of data obtained.

Evans, W. E. 1967 Vocalization among marine mammals. In: *Marine Bio-Acoustics*, Vol. II, pp. 159-186 (ed. W. N. Tavolga) Pergamon Press.

An account of the kinds of sounds produced by marine mammals with discussion of what is known regarding their significance.

Evans, W. E. 1967 Discussion of mechanisms of overcoming interference in echolocating animals, by A. D. Grinnell. In: *Animal Sonar Systems - Biology and Bionics*, Vol. 1, p. 495-503 (ed. R.-G. Busnel) Laboratoire de Physiologie Acoustique, Jouy-en-Josas 78, France.

Discusses some of the possible interference factors in biological echolocation in the aquatic environment.

Evans, W. E., and B. A. Powell 1967 Discrimination of different metallic plates by an echolocating delphinid. In: *Animal Sonar Systems - Biology and Bionics*, Vol. 1, pp. 366-383 (ed. R.-G. Busnel) Laboratoire de Physiologie Acoustiue, Jouy-en-Josas 78, France.

A bottlenose dolphin, blindfolded, was found to be capable of discriminating by echolocation a 30-cm diameter target (paddle) of 0.22 cm copper plate when paired with targets of other materials, including aluminum plate.

Evans, W. E., and J. Bastian 1969 Marine mammal communication; social and echological factors. In: *The Biology of Marine Mammals*, pp. 425-475 (ed. H. T. Andersen) Academic Press.

While many sounds made by marine mammals have social and communicative significance, there is not good evidence that porpoises (regarding which there has been much speculation) possess a language comparable to the human language.

Evans, W. E., and P. F. A. Maderson 1973 Mechanisms of sound production in delphinid cetaceans: A review and some anatomical considerations. Amer. Zool. *13*:1205-1213.

Review of earlier literature describing possible sites of sound-producing mechanisms, with a discussion of the morphology of the nasal sac system. It is concluded that theories implicating the nasal sac system in sound production are supported by certain anatomical specializations adjacent to the tissues of this system.

Evans, W. E. 1973 Echolocation by marine delphinids and one species of freshwater dolphin. Jour. Acoust. Soc. Am. *54*(1):191-199.

A brief summary of the state of knowledge of echolocation of small-toothed whales.

Fish, J. F., and H. E. Winn 1969 Sounds of marine mammals. In: *Encyclopedia of Marine Resources*, (ed. F. E. Firth) Van Nostrand Reinhold Co., pp. 649-655.

Summarizes important contributions to our knowledge of marine mammal sound production and hearing. Includes the major papers up to 1967.

Fish, J. F., and J. S. Vania 1971 Killer whale, *Orcinus orca*, sounds repel white whales. Fishery Bulletin *69*(3):531-535.

A study conducted to determine if white whales migrating up the Kvichak River in Alaska which feed on salmon smolt could be turned back by underwater transmission of killer whale sounds. The playback of killer whale sounds was found to be an effective way to keep white whales out of the river.

Fish, J. F., J. L. Sumich and G. L. Lingle 1974 Sounds produced by the gray whale, *Eschrichtius robustus*. Mar. Fish. Rev. *36*(4):38-48.

Describes the sounds recorded from a young gray whale in captivity and sounds recorded in the vicinity of the whale when it was returned to the ocean.

Fish, J. F., C. S. Johnson and D. K. Ljungblad 1976 Sonar target discrimination by instrumented human divers. Jour. Acoust. Soc. Am. *59*(3):602-606.

Human divers, instrumented with "bionic" sonar equipment based on the porpoise echolocation system and presented with targets earlier used in porpoise sonar discrimination experiments, made scores as good as or better than the porpoises had.

Fish, J. F., and C. W. Turl 1976 Acoustic source levels of four species of small whales. NUC TP 547, 14 pp.

   Absolute sound pressure level measurements were made at sea on herds of the common dolphin, pilot whale, bottlenose dolphin, and northern right whale dolphin.

Floyd, R. W. 1980 Models of cetacean signal processing. In: *Animal Sonar Systems*, pp. 615-623 (ed. R.-G. Busnel and J. F. Fish), Plenum Press.

   A review in which the apparent merits and deficiencies of various models of signal processing are discussed, with suggestions for future experiments.

Friedl, W. A., and P. O. Thompson 1981 Measuring acoustic noise around Kahoolawe Island. NOSC TR 732, 15 pp. (Also, abstract in Jour. Acoust. Soc. Am. Vol. 70, Suppl. 1, p. S84, 1981).

   Seven sonobuoys were monitored for seven hours from a P-3 aircraft during gunnery exercises by a Navy ship north of Kahoolawe. Humpback whale locations and behavior were also monitored. Whales were observed swimming, lying still, diving, surfacing, breeching, and lobtailing. Movements and activities of the whales could not be related to any airborne, surface, or subsurface stimuli.

Gales, R. S. 1966 Pickup, analysis and interpretation of underwater acoustic data. In: *Whales, Dolphins, and Porpoises*, (ed. K. S. Norris) Univ. of Calif. Press.

   Discusses instrumentation used for recording underwater sounds and presents analyses of a variety of cetacean sounds.

Green, R. F., S. H. Ridgway and W. E. Evans 1980 Functional and descriptive anatomy of the bottlenosed dolphin nasolaryngeal system with special reference to the musculature associated with sound production. In: *Animal Sonar Systems*, pp. 199-238 (ed. R.-G. Busnel and J. F. Fish), Plenum Press.

   Detailed anatomical information with reference to external landmarks to facilitate the use of electromyographic techniques in determining activity of specific muscles used in sound production.

Hall, J. D., and C. S. Johnson 1972 Auditory thresholds of a killer whale *Orcinus orca* Linnaeus. Jour. Acoust. Soc. Am. *51*(2, Pt. 2):515-517.

   Using operant conditioning techniques, an audiogram was obtained for a killer whale for frequencies between 500 Hz and 31 kHz. Greatest sensitivity was observed at 15 kHz, with upper limit of hearing at 32 kHz.

Hammer, Clifford, and W. W. L. Au 1978 Target recognition via echolocation by an Atlantic bottlenose dolphin (*Tursiops truncatus*). (Abstract) Jour. Acoust. Soc. Am. Vol. 64, Suppl. 1, p. S87.

Target-recognition behavior as a function of target composition and internal structure was investigated using cylindrical hollow aluminum and solid coral rock targets for baseline data. Experiments were then conducted to determine the critical characteristic for target recognition.

Hammer, C. E., and W. W. L. Au 1980 Porpoise echo-recognition: An analysis of controlling target characteristics. Jour. Acoust. Soc. Am. *68*(5):1285-1293.

After baseline performance was established, a two-alternative, forced-choice method with two hollow aluminum and two coral rock cylinders (standard targets), probe targets was used. The probe target results indicated that the bottlenose dolphin had learned to recognize the echo characteristics of the aluminum standards and differentiated other targets on that basis.

Jacobs, D. W., and J. D. Hall 1972 Auditory thresholds of a freshwater dolphin *Inia geoffrensis* Blainville. Jour. Acoust. Soc. Am. *51*(2, Pt. 2):530-533.

An Amazon River dolphin was conditioned to respond to pure tones by pushing a lever. By this method an audiogram was obtained for frequencies between between 1.0 and 105 kHz. Greatest sensitivity was found between 75 and 90 kHz, with effective upper limit of hearing at 105 kHz.

Johnson, C. S. 1967 The possible use of phase information in target discrimination, and the role of pulse rate in porpoise echoranging. In: *Animal Sonar Systems - Biology and Bionics*, Vol. 1, 384-398 (ed. R.-G. Busnel) Laboratoire de Physiologie Acoustique Jouy-en-Josas 78, France.

A discussion of the paper by Evans and Powell (see reference on page 7). On the basis of theoretical considerations there are phase differences in reflected pulse shapes which may be utilized by the porpoise. An analysis of pulse rate versus range and time indicates that decreasing pulse rate is based on time before target contact rather than range.

Johnson, C. S. 1968 Sound detection thresholds in marine mammals. In: *Marine Bio-Acoustics* Vol. 2, pp. 247-260 (ed. W. N. Tavolga) Pergamon Press.

By a behavioral response method, an audiogram for a bottlenose porpoise was obtained over a frequency range from 75 Hz to 150 kHz. Maximum sensitivity was found at about 50 kHz.

Johnson, C. S. 1968 Relation between absolute threshold and duration-of-tone pulses in the bottlenosed porpoise. Jour. Acoust. Soc. Am. *43*(4):757-763.

This study indicated that the porpoise, in detecting pure tone stimuli, integrated the acoustic energy in essentially the same way that humans do.

Johnson, C. S. 1969 Masked tonal thresholds in the bottlenosed porpoise. Jour. Acoust. Soc. Am. 44(4):965-967.

An analysis of hearing thresholds when a narrowband of frequencies is masked by broadband noise.

Johnson, C. S. 1970 Auditory masking of one pure tone by another in the bottlenosed porpoise. Jour. Acoust. Soc. Am. 48(5):7328.

Pure-tone masking-tone thresholds were obtained for a bottlenosed porpoise. Using a masking tone frequency of 70 kHz and masking levels at 40 and 80 dB above threshold, the shapes of the masking curves were similar to those obtained from human subjects at much lower frequencies.

Johnson, C. S. 1979 Thermal-noise limit in delphinid hearing. NOSC TD 270, pp. 1-4.

In quiet tanks thermal noise is the dominant sound source above 50 kHz. Evidence indicates that in the frequency range above 50 kHz cetacean auditory thresholds are limited by thermal noise.

Johnson, C. S. 1980 Important areas for future cetacean auditory study. In: *Animal Sonar Systems*, pp. 515-518 (ed. R.-G. Busnel and J. F. Fish), Plenum Press.

Discusses three apparent anomalies in experimental results on cetacean hearing.

Johnson, C. S. 1986 Dolphin audition and echolocation capacities. In: *Dolphin Cognition and Behavior*, pp. 115-136 (ed. R. J. Schusterman, J. A. Thomas, and F. G. Wood) Lawrence Erlbaum Associates.

A review. Includes ear anatomy and transduction mechanisms, auditory thresholds, echolocation sound production, and theoretical echolocation models.

Johnson, R. A. 1980 Energy spectrum analysis in echolocation. In: *Animal Sonar Systems*, pp. 673-693 (ed. R.-G. Busnel and J. F. Fish), Plenum Press.

Discusses object detection, distance estimation, and object identification and how they may be accomplished in energy spectrum analysis as an alternative to correlation processing in the time domain sense.

Kadane, James, R. H. Penner, W. W. L. Au, and R. W. Floyd 1980 Microprocessors in collection and analysis of *Tursiops truncatus* echolocation data. (Abstract) Jour. Acoust. Soc. Am. Vol. 68, Suppl. 1, p. S8.

Describes the equipment used to collect and analyze a variety of parameters of echolocation signals emitted by a dolphin in various detection tasks.

Kadane, James, and R. H. Penner 1983 Range ambiguity and pulse interval jitter in the bottlenose dolphin. Jour. Acoust. Soc. Am. *74*(3):1059-1061.

In pulse-mode sonar systems which use range gating, range ambiguity can be caused by echoes from objects at multiple distances returning simultaneously. A bottlenose dolphin was found to vary consecutive interpulse intervals enough to eliminate this form of range ambiguity.

Lang, T. G., and H. A. P. Smith 1965 Communication between dolphins in separate tanks by way of an acoustic link. Science *150*(3705):1839-1843.

Alternating exchange of different kinds of whistles occurred between two dolphins.

Ljungblad, D. K., and Stephen Leatherwood 1979 Sounds recorded in the presence of adult and calf bowhead whales, *Balaena mysticetus*. NOSC TR 420, Revision 1, pp. 1-8.

Low-frequency sounds, identified as Type A and Type B, were recorded. Type A sounds were of brief duration, with fundamental frequency ranging from 50 to 580 Hz and few or no harmonics. Type B sounds were longer, the fundamental frequency ranged from 100 to 195 Hz, and they were rich in harmonics.

Ljungblad, D. K., Stephen Leatherwood and M. E. Dahlheim 1980 Sounds recorded in the presence of an adult and calf bowhead whale. Mar. Fish. Rev. *42*(9-10):86-87.

Modified version of Ljungblad and Leatherwood 1979.

Ljungblad, D. K., P. D. Scoggins, and W. G. Gilmartin 1982 Auditory thresholds of a captive Eastern Pacific bottlenosed dolphin, *Tursiops* spp. Jour. Acoust. Soc. Am. *72*(6):1726-1729.

Hearing thresholds were tested using behavioral response techniques. The animal responded to signals ranging from 2 to 135 kHz, but not to higher frequencies. Range of greatest sensitivity was between 25 and 70 kHz, with peak sensitivities at 25 and 50 kHz.

Ljungblad, D. K., P. O. Thompson and S. E. Moore 1982 Underwater sounds recorded from migrating bowhead whales, *Balaena mysticetus*, in 1979. Jour. Acoust. Soc. Am. *71*(2):477-482.

Sounds were recorded from sonobuoys during spring and fall migrations. Most sounds at both times were low-frequency (below 800 Hz) moans, simple or complex. Repetitive sequences were found only in the spring samples. High-frequency (to 4 kHz) trumpeting calls were recorded in the fall (but also occurred in the spring of 1981).

Martin, D. W., and W. W. L. Au 1980 Aural discrimination of target echoes in white noise by human observers using broadband sonar pulses. (Abstract) Jour. Acoust Soc. Am. Vol. 68, Suppl. 1, p. S57.

Recordings of target echoes obtained from dolphin-like pulses directed at hollow aluminum and glass cylinders and one solid aluminum cylinder were played back to human subjects at 1/50 of the original rate. The average 75% correct response threshold occurred at different signal-to-noise ratios, with the lowest SNR for the solid target.

Martin, D. W., and W. W. L. Au 1983 Auditory detection of broadband sonar echoes from a sphere in white noise. (Abstract) Jour. Acoust. Soc. Am. Vol. 73, Suppl. 1, p. S91.

The ability of two human subjects to detect time-stretched broadband sonar echoes from a water-filled stainless-steel sphere in white noise was tested. At stretch factors of 75 and 50, the subjects performed better than dolphins did with unaltered echoes.

Martin, D. W., and W. W. L. Au 1986 Broadband sonar classification cues: An investigation. NOSC TR 1123, pp. 1-36.

Sonar echo-discrimination experiments were conducted with human subjects to (1) measure their performance using echoes from geometric targets, (2) determine the acoustic cues used, (3) develop software algorithms to extract echo features similar to those used by humans, and (4) determine whether the features can be used for automatic target classification.

McCormick, J. G., E. G. Wever, Jerry Palin and S. H. Ridgway 1971 Sound conduction in the dolphin ear. Jour. Acoust. Soc. Am. 48(6):1418-1428.

By electrophysiological methods, the mechanisms and pathways of sound conduction in the dolphin ear were determined.

McCormick, J. G., E. G. Wever, S. H. Ridgway and Jerry Palin 1980 Sound reception in the porpoise as it relates to echolocation. In: *Animal Sonar Systems*, pp. 449-467 (ed. R.-G. Busnel and J. F. Fish), Plenum Press.

A review of earlier work, with the addition of new information and arguments.

Moore, P. W. B., and W. W. L. Au 1975 Underwater localization of pulsed pure tones by the California Sea lion (*Zalophus californianus*). Jour. Acoust. Soc. Am. 58(3):721-727.

The animal appeared to use time-difference cues for lower frequencies (0.5-16 kHz) and intensity-difference cues for higher frequencies (4-16 kHz). The minimum auditory angles for the lower frequencies were smaller than for the higher frequencies.

Moore, P. W. B. 1980 Cetacean obstacle avoidance. In: *Animal Sonar Systems*, pp. 97-108 (ed. R.-G. Busnel and J. F. Fish), Plenum Press.

A review, including early dolphin echolocation experiments and field observations.

Moore, P. W. B., and W. W. L. Au 1981 Directional hearing sensitivity of the Atlantic bottlenose dolphin (*Tursiops truncatus*) in the vertical plane. (Abstract) Jour. Acoust. Soc. Am. Vol. 70, Suppl. 1, p. S85.

Maximum sensitivity for pure-tone frequencies of 30, 60, and 120 kHz occurred between 5 and 10 degrees above the midline of the mouth. Sensitivity dropped more sharply with increasing angle above the midline rather than below.

Moore, P. W. B., and W. W. L. Au 1982 Masked pure-tone thresholds of the bottlenosed dolphin (*Tursiops truncatus*) at extended frequencies. (Abstract) Jour. Acoust. Soc. Am. Vol. 70, Suppl. 1, p. S42.

Response thresholds at two masking noise levels were obtained from 30 to 140 kHz. The critical ratio (CR), ratios of signal power to noise spectrum level, was calculated for both noise levels. A function relating CRs to frequency conformed with previous finding to 100 kHz, but results above 100 kHz, not previously determined, showed a sharp increase at 110 kHz, followed by a decline at 120 kHz.

Moore, P. W. B., and W. W. L. Au 1983 Critical ratio and bandwidth of the Atlantic bottlenose dolphin (*Tursiops truncatus*). (Abstract) Jour. Acoust. Soc. Am. Vol. 74, Suppl. 1, p. S73.

Masked underwater pure-tone thresholds were obtained at test frequencies ranging from 30 to 140 kHz at two levels of broadband noise.

Moore, P. W. B., R. W. Hall, W. A. Friedl, and P. E. Nachtigall 1984 The critical interval in dolphin echolocation: What is it? Jour. Acoust. Soc. Am. *76*(1):314-317.

In an active echolocation target detection task, the echolocation click from a bottlenose dolphin triggered a short-sound-burst masking noise, from the target area, which could be adjusted from coincidence with the target echo to delays up to 700 μs. The animal's detection performance, high at long delays, dropped to chance level for a 100 μs delay. This was seen as supporting the view that time separation pitch may be an analytic mechanism used by the dolphin to discern within-echo target attributes rather than for determining target range.

Murchison, A. E. 1980 Detection range and range resolution of echolocating bottlenose porpoise (*Tursiops truncatus*). In: *Animal Sonar Systems*, pp. 43-70 (ed. R.-G. Busnel and J. F. Fish), Plenum Press.

The maximum detection ranges of two Tursiops were determined for two different spherical targets in open water. A third target was used to determine the effects of target depth (or nearness to the bottom) at maximum detection ranges.

Murchison, A. E., and S. A. Patterson 1980 The effect of extended reinforcement schedules on the receiver operating characteristics (ROC) of an echolocating Atlantic bottlenose dolphin (*Tursiops truncatus*). (Abstract) Jour. Acoust. Soc. Am. Vol. 68, Suppl. 1, p. S97.

After a dolphin was conditioned to report (by paddle press) presence or absence of a target, its performance was tested using different variable and fixed-ratio reinforcement schedules. The dolphin's ROC remained essentially unchanged for all schedules, but when it was kept on the more extended schedules for more than eight consecutive 100-trial sessions, all responses became "target absent."

Nachtigall, P. E. 1980 Odontocete echolocation performance on object size, shape and material. In: *Animal Sonar Systems*, pp. 71-95 (ed. R.-G. Busnel and J. F. Fish), Plenum Press.

A review.

Nachtigall, P. E. 1980 Bibliography of echolocation papers on aquatic mammals published between 1966 and 1978. In: *Animal Sonar Systems*, pp. 1029-1069 (ed. R.-G. Busnel and J. F. Fish), Plenum Press.

Lists 580 references, many from the Soviet literature.

Nachtigall, P. E., and S. A. Patterson 1980 Echolocation sameness-difference discrimination by the Atlantic bottlenose dolphin (*Tursiops truncatus*). (Abstract) Jour. Acoust Soc. Am. Vol. 68, Suppl. 1, p. S98.

A dolphin was trained to respond differentially to two simultaneously presented stimulus objects, depending on whether they were identical or different. After development of the sameness-difference concept, novel stimuli were similarly presented, and following successful completion of this test, sensory modality transfer was also achieved when the animal was blindfolded with rubber eyecups.

Nachtigall, P. E., A. E. Murchison and W. W. L. Au 1980 Cylinder and cube shape discrimination by an echolocating blindfolded bottlenosed dolphin. In: *Animal Sonar Systems*, pp. 945-947 (ed. R.-G. Busnel and J. F. Fish), Plenum Press. (Also, abstract in Jour. Acoust. Soc. Am. Vol. 64, Suppl. 1, p. S87-1978).

The dolphin could discriminate the cylinder as its aspect was changed except when the flat top of the cylinder faced the animal. Acoustic examination of the targets failed to reveal consistent and obvious echo cues for the discrimination of shape, but replicated measurements of target strength for each target revealed differences in standard deviations that paralleled the performance of the animal.

Northrop, J., W. C. Cummings and P. O. Thompson 1968 20-Hz Signals observed in the Central Pacific. Jour. Acoust. Soc. Am. *43*(2):383-384.

20-Hz signals recorded in the mid-Pacific area had source levels that ranged from 65 to 100 dB re 1 microbar at 1 yd. The original strength, source movement, and seasonal peak suggested the sounds were from a biological source, probably the finback whale.

15

Northrop, J., W. C. Cummings and M. F. Morrison 1971 Underwater 20-Hz signals recorded near Midway Island. Jour. Acoust. Soc. Am. *49*(6, Pt. 2):1909-1910.

This paper describes doublets of 25 sec., 20-Hz signals believed to be from whales. Signals occurred in trains of source levels ranging from 53 to 71 dB re 1 microbar at 1 yd.

Penner, R. H., and A. E. Murchison 1970 Experimentally demonstrated echolocation in the Amazon River porpoise, *Inia geoffrensis*. NUC TP 187, 28 pp.

An analysis of the ability of a freshwater porpoise to discriminate, by echolocation, wires or tubes of different diameters.

Penner, R. H., and James Kadane 1980 *Tursiops* biosonar detection in noise. In: *Animal Sonar Systems*, pp. 957-959 (ed. R.-G. Busnel and J. F. Fish), Plenum Press.

In a detection problem in a high ambient noise environment with presentation of white noise at five different levels, the overall performance of two *Tursiops* degraded as noise level increased. The click count ("echolocation effort") and response latency both increased until the noise exceeded 77 dB. At the two highest levels, 82 and 87 dB, the click trains became shorter and latencies were longer.

Penner, R. H., and J. Kadane 1980 Biosonar interpulse interval as an indicator of attending distance in *Tursiops truncatus*. (Abstract) Jour. Acoust. Soc. Am. Vol. 80, Suppl. 1, p. S97.

In a biosonar detection study, the relationship between interpulse interval lengths and calculated acoustical two-way travel time was found to describe an attending distance appropriate to the distance between animal and target.

Penner, R. H., and C. W. Turl 1983 Bottlenose dolphin (*Tursiops truncatus*): Difference in the pattern of interpulse intervals. (Abstract) Jour. Acoust. Soc. Am. Vol. 74, Suppl. 1, p. S74.

When the echolocation detection abilities of a bottlenose dolphin and a beluga were tested on identical targets at the same distances, their interpulse-interval distributions differed, but detection accuracy was not significantly different.

Penner, R. H., C. W. Turl, and W. W. L. Au 1986 Target detection by the beluga using a surface-reflected path. Jour. Acoust. Soc. Am. *80*:1842-1843.

During an echolocation-in-noise experiment, a beluga was suspected of using a surface-reflected path to maximize detection performance. Tests confirmed this suspicion.

Powell, B. A. 1966 Periodicity of vocal activity of captive Atlantic bottlenose dolphins, *Tursiops truncatus*. Bull. So. Calif. Acad. Sci. *65*(4):237-244.

Periodicity of vocal activity was found to be related to feeding periods and could be altered by changing the feeding schedule.

Ridgway, S. H., D. A. Carder, R. F. Green, A. S. Gaunt, S. L. L. Gaunt, and W. E. Evans 1980 Electromyographic and pressure events in the nasolaryngeal system of dolphins during sound production. In: *Animal Sonar Systems*, pp. 239-249 (ed. R.-G. Busnel and J. F. Fish), Plenum Press.

Study of the gross and microanatomical nature of the nasal plug nodes, diagonal membrane, and nasofrontal sacs, coupled with acoustic, electromyographic, and pressure measurements strongly indicated that this system constitutes the source of sound production. The data show no evidence for sound production in the larynx.

Ridgway, S. H. 1980 Electrophysiological experiments on hearing in odontocetes. In: *Animal Sonar Systems*, pp. 483-493 (ed. R.-G. Busnel and J. F. Fish), Plenum Press.

A review.

Ridgway, S. H. 1983 Dolphin hearing and sound production in health and illness. In: *Hearing and Other Senses: Presentations in Honor of E. G. Wever*, pp. 247-296 (ed. R. R. Fay and G. Gourevitch), Amphora Press.

Review of findings on dolphin hearing, with accounts of modern anatomic and physiologic work on the ear; the brain, evoked potentials, and audition; and evidence that sound production can be used to assess dolphin health and mood.

Ridgway, S. H., and D. A. Carder 1983 Audiograms for large cetaceans: A proposed method for field studies. (Abstract) Jour. Acoust. Soc. Am. Vol. 74, Suppl. 1, p. S53.

Audiograms for small cetaceans have been produced by the averaged-brainstem-response technique using EEGs recorded when sound pulses are presented via a hydrophone. It is proposed that this technique could be used to obtain audiograms from large whales that have become trapped, stranded, or beached.

Ridgway, S. H. 1983 Dolphin sound production: Physiologic, diurnal, and behavioral correlations. (Abstract) Jour. Acoust. Soc. Am. Vol. 74, Suppl. 1, p. S73.

Identifies unanswered questions regarding mechanics of dolphin sound production and states findings on correlations identified in the title.

Schusterman, R. J., R. F. Balliet and James Nixon 1972 Underwater audiogram of the California sea lion by the conditioned vocalization technique. Jour. Exper. Anal. Behavior *17*:339-350.

Conditioned vocalizations were used to obtain underwater sound detection thresholds at ranges from 250 to 64,000 Hz. Maximum sensitivity was between 1 and 28 kHz. With relatively intense acoustic signals, Zalophus will respond to frequencies at least as high as 192 kHz.

Schusterman, R. J., Barry Barrett, and Patrick Moore 1975 Detection of underwater signals by a California sea lion and a bottlenose porpoise: variation in the payoff matrix. Jour. Acoust. Soc. Am. *57*(6, Pt. 2):1526-1532.

Results indicated that varying the payoff matrix (number of fish given for correct performance) may be an effective way to control response bias in experiments dealing with the detection of underwater signals by marine mammals.

Schusterman, R. J. 1980 Behavioral methodology in echolocation by marine mammals. In: *Animal Sonar Systems*, pp. 11-41 (ed. R.-G. Busnel and J. F. Fish), Plenum Press.

A comprehensive review of methodology and experimental design in echolocation studies of marine mammals.

Schusterman, R. J., D. A Kersting, and W. W. L. Au 1980 Response bias and attention in discriminative echolocation by Tursiops truncatus. In: *Animal Sonar Systems*, pp. 983-986 (ed. R.-G. Busnel and J. F. Fish), Plenum Press.

Describes an experiment testing the notion that a response bias acquired in an insolvable discriminative echolocation task will strongly influence the attention of a dolphin in a similar but solvable task. The results indicated that this happened.

Schusterman, R. J., and P. W. B. Moore 1980 Auditory sensitivity of northern fur seals (*Callorhinus ursinus*) and a California sea lion (*Zalophus californianus*) to airborne sound. (Abstract) Jour. Acoust. Soc. Am. Vol. 68, Suppl. 1, p. S6.

At even frequencies, from 1 to 30 kHz, the thresholds, although inferior in air compared to water, showed good accommodation for hearing airborne sounds. The otariic pinnipeds appear to be more sensitive to airborne sounds than do the phocid pininipeds.

Schusterman, R. J., D. A. Kersting and W. W. L. Au 1980 Stimulus control of echolocation pulses in *Tursiops truncatus*. In: *Animal Sonar Systems*, pp. 981-982 (ed. R.-G. Busnel and J. F. Fish), Plenum Press.

A major problem in determining what cue or set of cues a dolphin uses in target detection or discrimination has been the ambiguous nature of the echo return relative to the position of the dolphin. In this experiment the problem was solved by training the dolphin to position precisely and emit echolocation pulses on cue.

Scronce, B. L., and C. S. Johnson 1975 Bistatic target detection by a bottlenosed porpoise. Jour. Acoust. Soc. Am. *59*(4):1001-1002.

The porpoise was acoustically masked to prevent use of its echolocation pulses and trained to report the presence or absence of a 7.62-cm-diam. hollow stainless steel sphere by listening. The sphere was ensonified by a broadband, click-type pulse.

Scronce, B. L., and S. H. Ridgway 1980 Grey seal, *Halichoerus*: echolocation not demonstrated. In: *Animal Sonar Systems*, pp. 991-993 (ed. R.-G. Busnel and J. F. Fish), Plenum Press.

A gray seal, trained to wear a blindfold, was tested for echolocation capability in detection and discrimination tasks. Successful detection of an air-filled ring occurred with and without head scanning and emission of click trains, suggesting that the ring was a good passive target. Performance in a discrimination task was at a chance level.

Scronce, B. L., and S. H. Ridgway 1983 Seal blindfolded discrimination: Echolocation not proven in *Halichoerus grypus*. (Abstract) Jour. Acoust. Soc. Am. Vol. 74, Suppl. 1, p. S75.

Experiments with a gray seal trained to wear an opaque band that blocked vision provided no evidence of an echolocation capability.

Thompson, P. O. 1965 Deep water recordings of pinniped sounds. Addendum to Proc. 2nd Conf. Biol. Sonar and Diving Mammals, 11 pp, Stanford Research Institute, Menlo Park, California.

Describes, in detail, underwater recordings of barking sounds from California sea lions off San Clemente Island. Diurnal characteristics, spectrum plots, and sonograms are included.

Thompson, P. O., and W. C. Cummings 1969 Sound production of the finback whale, *Balaeoptera physalus*, and Eden's whale *B. edeni*, in the Gulf of California. (Abstract) Proc. 6th Conf. Biol. Sonar and Diving Mammals, Stanford Research Institute, p. 109.

Describes powerful, low-frequency sounds from two species of whales found in the Gulf of California. Finback signals ranges from 20-100 Hz, while those from Eden's whale averaged 124 Hz. Although finbacks have been suspected as sources of 20-Hz signals, these were not encountered among the 1800 phonations recorded from some 70 finbacks.

Thompson, P. O. 1978 Underwater repetitive mammal sound sequences in the Bering Strait. (Abstract) Jour. Acoust. Soc. Am. Vol. 64, Suppl. 1, p. S87.

Sounds similar to but simpler than the "songs" of the humpback whale were recorded. Among possible sources were the walrus and the bowhead whale.

Thompson, P. O., and W. A. Friedl 1982 A long-term study of low frequency sounds from several species of whales off Oahu, Hawaii. Cetology No. 45, 19 pp.

Two bottom-mounted hydrophones were monitored from December 1978 through April 1981. Sounds of five whale species (humpback, fin, blue, sperm, and pilot) were identified. The "boing" sound was also recorded. Sounds were received most frequently in winter and spring, least frequently in July and October.

Turl, C. W., and R. H. Penner   1983   Target detection: Beluga whale and bottlenose dolphin echolocation abilities compared.   (Abstract)   Jour. Acoust. Soc. Am. Vol. 74, Suppl. 1, p. S74.

No significant difference in performance was found for five targets of the same size and target strength at distances of 40 to 120 m.

Wenz, G. M.   1964   Curious noises and the sonic environment in the ocean.   In: *Marine Bio-Acoustics*, Vol. 1, pp. 101-119 (ed. Wm. N. Tavolga) Pergamon Press.

Describes ambient noise of the ocean—from waves, precipitation, earthquakes, ships, marine organisms, etc.—and discusses certain noises of biological origin, including some whose sources had not been identified.

Wever, E. G., J. G. McCormick, Jerry Palin and S. H. Ridgway   1971   The cochlea of the dolphin, *Tursiops truncatus*:   Hair cells and ganglion cells.   Proc. Nat. Acad. Sci. USA *68*(12):2908-2912.

The large number of hair cells found suggests a high order of auditory proficiency, and the large ratio of ganglion cells to hair cells suggests an unusual ability to utilize auditory information.

Wever, E. G., J. G. McCormick, Jerry Palin and S. H. Ridgway   1971   The cochlea of the dolphin, *Tursiops truncatus*:   General morphology.   Proc. Nat. Acad. Sci. USA *68*(10):2381-2385.

Describes the microscopic structure of the cochlea and discusses features believed to represent adaptations for the reception of high-frequency sounds.

Wever, E. G., J. C. McCormick, Jerry Palin and S. H. Ridgway   1971   Cochlea of the dolphin, *Tursiops truncatus*:   The basilar membrane.   Proc. Nat. Acad. Sci. USA *68*(11):2708-2711.

Describes the microscopic structure of the basilar membrane and notes features suggesting unusual capabilities of pitch discrimination at very high frequencies.

Wever, E. G., J. G. McCormick, Jerry Palin and S. H. Ridgway   1972   Cochlear structure in the dolphin, *Langenorhynchus obliquidens*.   Proc. Nat. Acad. Sci. USA *69*(3):657-661.

Describes the microscope structure of the cochlea and discusses the significance of cell numbers in the hearing of *Langenorhynchus*.

Wood, F. G., and W. E. Evans 1980 Adaptiveness and ecology of echolocation in toothed whales. In: *Animal Sonar Systems*, pp. 381-425 (ed. R.-G. Busnel and J. F. Fish), Plenum Press.

Review of echolocation signal characteristics of various toothed whales with respect to their different ecological niches, foods, behaviors, etc. It is proposed that certain asymmetrical features (skull, narial system) are related to the development of a sonar system. Differences in relative brain size appear to correspond to degree of adaptibility, sensory integration, and versatility of sonar system.

See also Cummings, Thompson, and Fish, 1974, in the BEHAVIOR section.

2. PHYSIOLOGY/ANATOMY/GROWTH AND AGING

Bello, M. A., R. R. Roy, T. P. Martin, H. W. Goforth, Jr., and V. R. Edgerton 1985 Axial musculature in the dolphin (*Tursiops truncatus*): Some architectural and histochemical characteristics. Mar. Mamm. Sci. *1*:324-336.

In view of reports that dolphins can swim faster than would be predicted based on physical features and presumed muscle power, this study examined muscle fiber types, fiber sizes, and tendon arrangements of the dorsal and ventral axial muscles.

Brown, W. R., J. R. Geraci, B. D. Hicks, D. J. St. Aubin, and J. P. Schroeder 1983 Epidermal cell proliferation in the bottlenose dolphin (*Tursiops truncatus*). Canadian Jour. Zool. *61*:1587-1590.

Using a radioactive labeling technique, the authors found that *Tursiops* has a large proliferative capacity which contributes to the unusual thickness of the skin.

Ceruti, M. G. 1983 Chemical characteristics of compounds released by marine mammals. NOSC TR 930, 52 pp.

Excretions, secretions, and glandular extracts were analyzed to determine chemical constituents which may be involved in marine mammal chemoreception.

Ceruti, M. G., P. V. Fennessey, and S. S. Tjoa 1985 Chemoreceptively active compounds in secretions, excretions and tissue extracts of marine mammals. Comp. Biochem. Physiol. *32A*:505-514.

Hypothesizing that chemical communication may occur in marine mammals and that analysis of secretions and excretions would identify some specific compounds that might be involved, the authors determined the principal chemical components of sexual secretions, urine, feces, and blood from Atlantic *Tursiops*. Twenty-two identified compounds in aqueous solutions of sufficient concentration could be detected gustatorily by humans.

Coulombe, H. N., S. H. Ridgway and W. E. Evans 1965 Respiratory water exchange in two species of porpoise. Science *149*(3679):86-88.

The exhalations of the two species of porpoises examined contained less water vapor than those of terrestrial mammals. This is seen as an adaptation to conserve water in these animals which live in an environment where no fresh water is available.

Dawson, W. W., D. A. Carder, S. H. Ridgway and E. T. Schmeisser 1981 Synchrony of dolphin eye movements and their power density spectra. Comp. Biochem. Physiol. *68A*:443-339.

Eye movements in the horizontal and vertical planes of a normal human and two bottlenose dolphins were analyzed and compared. Although dolphin eyes are mobile at lower fundamental frequencies than in humans, there is a low level of synchrony between the two eyes.

Dawson, W. W., J. P. Schroeder, and J. F. Dawson 1987 The ocular fundus of two cetaceans. Mar. Mamm. Sci. *3*:1-13.

By use of a technique to correct the aerial myopia encountered in fundus photography of the marine mammal eye, the first high quality photographs were obtained of the eyes of living *Tursiops* and a *Grampus*.

Dawson, W. W., J. P. Schroeder, and S. N. Sharpe 1987 Corneal surface properties of two marine mammal species. Mar. Mamm. Sci. *3*:186-197.

Describes and compares the cornea of *Tursiops* and *Zalophus*. The results provide an explanation for the resolution of the *Zalophus* eye in air and water, but "the aerial acuity of *Tursiops* remains a mystery."

Evans, W. E. 1974 Telemetering of temperature and depth data from a free-ranging yearling California gray whale, *Eschrichtius robustus*. Mar. Fish. Rev. 36(4):52-58.

A young female gray whale which had been held in captivity for a year was released carrying a radiotelemetry package which transmitted depth of dive and temperature-at-depth data.

Flanigan, N. J. 1965 Neuroanatomy of the dolphin spinal cord. Anat. Rec. *151*:350.

Flanigan, N. J. 1966 The anatomy of the spinal cord of the Pacific whitesided dolphin, *Langenorhynchus obliquidens*. In: *Whales, Dolphins, and Porpoises*, pp. 207-231 (ed. K. S. Norris) U. of Calif. Press.

Describes the anatomy of the spinal cord and discusses the possible significance of its distinctive features.

Flanigan, N. J. 1972 The central nervous system. In: *Mammals of the Sea - Biology and Medicine*, pp. 215-246 (ed. S. H. Ridgway) Chas. C. Thomas, Publisher.

Reviews present knowledge of the central nervous system of cetaceans and pinnipeds, including findings made by the author while working at the Navy's Marine Bioscience Facility.

Gilmartin, W. G., R. W. Pierce, and G. A. Antonelis, Jr. 1974 Some physiological parameters of the blood of the California gray whale. Mar. Fish. Rev. 36(4):28-31.

Hematocrit, oxyhemoglobin dissociation curve, and blood volume were determined, the last by isotopic techniques.

Green, R. F. 1972 Observations on the anatomy of some cetaceans and pinnipeds. In: *Mammals of the Sea - Biology and Medicine*, pp. 247-297 (ed. S. H. Ridgway) Chas. C. Thomas, Publisher.

Observations (with unique new illustrations) of cetacean and pinniped anatomy based primarily on dissections made by the author.

Greenwood, A. G., S. H. Ridgway and R. J. Harrison 1971 Blood values in young gray seals. Jour. Am. Vet. Med. Assn. *159*(5):571-574.

Red and white blood cell measurements, plasma electrolytes and serum proteins, and blood chemistry values are given.

Hamlin, R. L., et al. 1972 Electrocardiogram of pinnipeds. Am. Jour. Vet. Res. *33*(4):867-875.

Electrocardiograms obtained from California sea lions, elephant seals, and harbor seal are analyzed and discussed.

Harrison, R. J., and S. H. Ridgway 1971 Gonadal activity in some bottlenose dolphins (*Tursiops trunactus*). Jour. Zool., London *165*:355-366.

Characteristics of the ovaries and testes of young and adult bottlenose dolphins indicate that sexual maturity in females is probably reached in their fifth year. Males become sexually mature at an estimated age of ten years. No evidence of regular cyclic ovulation was found.

Harrison, R. J., and S. H. Ridgway 1972 Telemetry in experimental and trained dives by seals. Proc. Anat. Soc. Gr. Brit. and Ireland, Jour. Anat. *111*(3):491.

See last item above.

Harrison, R. J., and S. H. Ridgway 1972 Seals, dolphins, and diving. New Scientist, 10 August 1972, pp. 283-285.

Describes how diving responses can be monitored by radiotelemetry.

Harrison, R. J., S. H. Ridgway and P. L. Joyce 1972 Telemetry of heart rate in seals. Nature *238*:280.

Radiotelemetry devices were implanted in the hypodermis of the neck and back of gray seals to follow heart-rate changes in unrestrained seals diving on command. Bradycardia was found to be less marked during trained dives than in previously reported forced and restrained dives.

Harrison, R. J., and S. H. Ridgway 1975 Restrained and unrestrained diving in seals. Rapp. p.-v. Reun. Cons. Int. Explor. Mer. *169*:76-80.

Cardiovascular response of gray seals was much higher diving a forced dive than during an unrestrained trained dive. Cardiac rhythm also varied with different observed behaviors.

Harrison, R. J., and S. H. Ridgway 1976 Deep Diving Mammals. 51 pp. Meadowfield Press Ltd., Durham, England.

A booklet reviewing what is known about deep diving in mammals, including depth and duration of dives, historical background, adaptations, other aspects of deep diving, and future deep diving by man.

25

Horvath, S. M., H. Chiodi, S. H. Ridgway and S. Azar, Jr. 1968 Respiratory and electrophoretic characteristics of hemoglobin of porpoises and sea lions. Comp. Biochem. Physiol. *24*:1027-1033.

Porpoises which swim faster and dive longer and deeper have greater hemoglobin oxygen affinity than the slower-swimming, shallower and shorter-diving species.

Hui, C. A., 1975 Thoracic collapse as affected by the *retia thoracica* in the dolphin. Resp. Physiol. *25*:63-70 (Netherlands).

The carcass of a *Delphinus* was subjected to two simulated dives in a hyperbaric chamber to the equivalent of 69.7 m. In one dive the thorax was in natural state, in the other 100 ml of water had been injected into each pleural cavity. Results indicated that an engorged thoracicrete reduces the displacement stress on abdominal organs under pressures encountered in diving.

Hui, C. A. 1978 Reliability of using dentin layers for age determination in *Tursiops truncatus*. Report to Marine Mammal Commission. Nat'l Tech. Info. Serv. PB-288 444, 25 pp.

Discusses histology of the mammalian tooth, utility of using dentin layers for age determination, and findings from an examination of teeth from three *Tursiops*, two of known age. It is concluded that annual increments of dentin are visible and can be regular through 11 years. No correlation of dentin layering with food consumption patterns or innate biorythms based on lunar cycles was found.

Hui, C. A. 1979 Correlates of maturity in the common dolphin, *Delphinus delphis*. Fish. Bull. *77*:295-300.

Body weight and length, degree of bone fusion in flippers, dentine layers, testis weights, and ovarian scars in 87 *D. delphis* (which had died in tuna nets) were treated statistically to determine correlation with sexual maturity.

Hui, C. A. 1981 Seawater consumption and water flux in the common dolphin *Delphinus delphis*. Physiol. Zool. *54*(4):430-440.

In two captive dolphins total body water was found to be low (37% of total body weight), indicating a high fractional rate of water turnover, most of which is due to the permeability of the skin. Skin was shown to be impermeable to sodium, so the only sodium source is ingested sea water.

Kanwisher, J. W., and S. H. Ridgway 1983 The physiological ecology of whales and porpoises. Sci. Am. *248*(6):110-120.

Discusses the particular physiologic adaptations evolved by cetaceans for living in the sea, notably the ability to dive deep for long periods. Unlike other marine organisms, which tend to move nutrients downward, oceanic marine mammals, through their fecal output near the surface, tend to move nutrients upward.

Leatherwood, Stephen, M. W. Deerman and C. W. Potter 1978 Food and reproductive status of nine *Tursiops truncatus* from the northeastern United States coast. Cetology No. 28, 6 pp.

The nine dolphins (six stranded, three entangled in a fishing net) were examined for age, reproductive status, and stomach contents. Stomachs contained a predominance of Atlantic croakers, sea trout, and spot.

Lowell, W. R., and W. F. Flanigan, Jr. 1978 Chemoreception in marine mammals: A review of the literature. NOSC TR 353, 19 pp.

Discusses anatomical and physiological correlates and behavioral and ecological considerations of olfaction and gustation in cetaceans, pinnipeds, sea otters, and sirenians, followed by a bibliography. (See also a later version, Marine Mammal Chemoreception, Mamm. Rev. *10*:53-59, 1980.)

Malvin, R. L., J.-P. Bonjous and S. H. Ridgway 1971 Antidiuretic hormone levels in some cetaceans. Proc. Soc. Exp. Biol. and Med. *136*(4):1203-1205.

Data on renal function in the bottlenose dolphin and killer whale are presented and discussed.

Malvin, R. L., S. H. Ridgway and Lanny Cornell 1978 Renin and aldosterone levels in dolphins and sea lions. Proc. Soc. Exper. Biol. and Med. *157*:665-668.

A significant correlation between plasma renin activity (PRA) and concentration of aldosterone in plasma was found in both dolphins and sea lions. An excellent correlation between urinary sodium excretion and PRA was also obtained in two dolphins. These data support the hypothesis that in marine mammals the renin-angiotension-aldosterone axis plays a role in the regulation of salt balance.

McCormick, J. G., E. G. Wever, J. L. Mattsson, and S. H. Ridgway 1977 Anatomical and physiological adaptations of marine mammals for the prevention of diving-induced middle-ear barotrauma and round window fistula. Undersea Biomedical Research *4*(1):A 42.

Comparative marine mammal experience helped make a preoperative diagnosis of diving-induced round window fistula in a human patient.

Nachtigall, P. E., and R. W. Hall 1984 Taste reception in the bottlenosed dolphin. Acta Zool. Fennica *172*:147-148.

A dolphin's taste thresholds for citric acid (sour) and quinine sulfate (bitter) were found to be just above the human thresholds for these substances.

Nachtigall, P. E. 1986 Vision, audition, and chemoreception in dolphins and other marine mammals. In: *Dolphin Cognition and Behavior*, pp. 79-113 (ed. R. J. Schusterman, J. A. Thomas, and F. G. Wood) Lawrence Erlbaum Associates.

A review of what is known about sensory capabilities in dolphins, pinnipeds, and sea otters (vision only).

Pepper, R. L., and J. V. Simmons, Jr. 1973 In-air visual acuity of the bottlenose dolphin. Exper. Neur. *41*(2):271-276.

Horizontal black and white line gratings were presented in a successive discrimination task. Over a constant viewing distance of 2.8 m, a minimal visual angle of 18 min. of arc was obtained.

Ridgway, S. H., and D. G. Johnston 1966 Blood oxygen and ecology of porpoises of three genera. Science *151*(3709):456-458.

The total blood-oxygen content of the highly active, deep-diving Dall's porpoise is almost three times that of the coastal dwelling bottlenose. The pelagic white-sided dolphin, less active than the Dall, is intermediate. Heart weight of the Dall's porpoise is about 140 percent that of the bottlenose.

Ridgway, S. H., B. L. Scronce and J. Kanwisher 1969 Respiration and deep diving in the bottlenose porpoise. Science *166*:1651-1654.

A porpoise was trained to dive on command to depths down to 300 m, then provide a lung air sample at the surface before breathing. It was also trained to swim between divers at 20 m and to breath-hold at the surface for deep-dive time equivalents. Analyses of oxygen and carbon dioxide were then compared for the three situations.

Ridgway, S. H., J. G. Simpson, G. S. Patton, and W. G. Gilmartin 1970 Hematologic findings in certain small cetaceans. Jour. Am. Vet. Med. Assn. *157*:566-575.

Clinical laboratory data on the blood of small cetaceans were collected from representatives of a number of species.

Ridgway, S. H., and G. S. Patton 1971 Dolphin thyroid: Some anatomical and physiological findings. Z. vergl. Physiol. *71*:129-141.

Research conducted with representatives of four species of delphinid was directed toward elucidating the function of this organ in toothed cetaceans. Biochemical data on thyroid hormones are presented. All of the animals examined had larger thyroids than terrestrial mammals of comparable weight.

Ridgway, S. H. 1971 Buoyancy regulation in deep diving whales. Nature *232*(5306):133-134.

Comments on a suggestion that the spermaceti organ of sperm whales serves as a buoyancy regulator in deep dives. Evidence is presented that this hypothesis is incorrect.

Ridgway, S. H., 1972 Homeostasis in the aquatic environment. In: *Mammals of the Sea - Biology and Medicine*, pp. 590-747 (ed. S. H. Ridgway) Chas. C. Thomas, Publisher.

Account of marine mammal research conducted by the author in the areas of diving physiology, water balance, reproductive physiology, hematology and blood chemistry, husbandry, behavior, and animal health (including anesthesia).

Ridgway, S. H. 1973 Control mechanisms in diving dolphins and seals. Doctoral Thesis, University of Cambridge, 90 pp. with appendices.

Primarily on diving physiology of dolphins, sea lions, and seals (espcially the gray seal), but also includes research on hearing, sleep, and brain temperatures in the grey seal.

Ridgway, S. H., J. G. McCormick and E. G. Wever 1974 Surgical approach to the dolphin's ear. Jour. Exp. Pathol. *188*(3):265-276.

Describes anesthesia procedure, surgical techniques, and physiological monitoring for making electrophysiological measurements at the cochlea.

Ridgway, S. H., D. A. Carder and William Clark 1975 Conditioned bradicardia in the sea lion *Zalophus californianus*. Nature *256*(5512):37-38.

Slowing of heart rate was achieved by conventional conditioning techniques.

Ridgway, S. H., and R. J. Harrison and P. L. Joyce 1975 Sleep and cardiac rhythm in the gray seal. Science *187*:553-555.

Brainwaves, heartbeat, and eye movements of seals sleeping underwater, on the surface, or when hauled out were recorded by radiotelemetry.

Ridgway, S. H., and P. L. Joyce 1975 Studies on seal brain by radiotelemetry. Rapp. P.-v. Reun. Cons. Int. Explor. Mer *169*:81-91.

Auditory-evoked potentials of the gray seal were used to obtain evoked response curves for auditory stimulation. Cortical-evoked response was most sensitive at 4 kHz in air and at 20-25 kHz underwater. Also includes EEG and EKG data on sleep in the grey seal, with observations of behavior.

Ridgway, S. H. 1976 Diving mammals and biomedical research. Oceanus *19*(2):49-55.

Describes biomedical research conducted with the California sea lion, gray seal, common seal, elephant seal, Weddell seal and bottlenose dolphin.

Ridgway, S. H., and R. H. Brownson 1979 Brain size and symmetry in three dolphin genera. Anat. Rec. *193*:664.

Asymmetries of weight and surface area of cerebral cortex between right and left hemispheres were found in *Tursiops* and *Delphinus*, but no significant asymmetries were found in *Stenella*. Average body and brain weights, lengths, and cortical surface areas are given for 13 *Tursiops*, 9 *Delphinus*, and 11 *Stenella*.

Ridgway, S. H., and Red Howard 1979 Dolphin lung collapse and intramuscular circulation during free diving: Evidence from nitrogen washout. Science 206:1182-1183.

Intramuscular nitrogen tensions in *Tursiops* after repetitive ocean dives suggested that lung collapse occurs at a depth of about 70 meters and that intramuscular circulation is maintained during unrestrained diving in the open sea. The dolphin is not protected by lung collapse in dives shallower than 70 meters.

Ridgway, S. H., T. H. Bullock, D. A. Carder, R. L. Seeley, D. Woods, and R. Galambos 1981 Auditory brainstem responses in dolphins. Proc. Natl. Acad. Sci. 78(3):1943-1947.

Auditory brainstem response (ABR) in two *Tursiops* and two *Delphinus* were compared with human and rat ABR data. The ABR can be used to test theories of dolphin sonar signal processing and permits rapid evaluation of hearing thresholds. Audiometric information on stranded or trapped giant whales might be obtained by using the ABR.

Ridgway, S. H., and C. A. Fenner 1982 Weight-length relationships of wild-caught and captive Atlantic bottlenose dolphins. Jour. Am Vet. Med. Assn. 181(11):1310-1315.

From weight and length measurements of 144 dolphins, guidelines were established for use in estimating whether a dolphin is over- or underweight.

Ridgway, S. H., C. A. Bowers, D. Miller, M. L. Schultz, C. A. Jacobs, and C. A. Dooley 1984 Diving and blood oxygen in the white whale. Canadian Jour. Zool. 62(11):2349-2351.

White whales, trained to dive on command in the open sea, remained submerged as long as 15 min 50 sec and dove as deep as 647 m (2122 ft).

Ridgway, S. H., and R. H. Brownson 1984 Relative brain sizes and cortical surface areas in odontocetes. Acta Zool. Fennica 172:149-152.

Surface area of the cerebral cortex was found to be directly related to brain weight in a variety of odontocetes, but the genera differed greatly when cortical area and brain weight were related to body length and weight and to encephalization quotient. Includes findings on brains of neonates and on brain asymmetries.

Ridgway, S. H. 1986 Diving dolphins. In: *Research on Dolphins*, pp. 33-58 (ed. M. M. Bryden and Richard Harrison) Clarendon Press, Oxford.

Includes historical background on depth-of-dive inferences and observations, modern studies, hazards of diving, respiration, bradycardia, and species differences with respect to metabolism, blood volume, and blood oxygen capacity.

Ridgway, S. H. 1986 Dolphin brain size. In: *Research on Dolphins*, pp. 59-70 (ed. M. M. Bryden and R. J. Harrison) Oxford University Press.

Discusses absolute brain sizes in cetaceans; the various cephalization coefficient concepts, including Jerison's "encephalization quotient," here applied to cetaceans; growth of the brain; fissurization; volume of the dolphin cortex; and asymmetry of the dolphin brain.

Ridgway, S. H. 1986 Diving in cetaceans. In: *Diving in Animals and Man*, pp. 33-62 (ed. A. O. Brubakk, J. W. Kanwisher, and G. Sundness) The Norwegian Society of Science and Letters, Trondheim, Norway.

A comprehensive account, including known diving capabilities of 10 cetaceans, techniques used to study diving, physiological and anatomical hazards of diving, adaptations for diving, sound production and diving, metabolism and diving, oxygen stores, and bradycardia.

Ridgway, S. H. 1986 Physiological observations on dolphin brains. In: *Dolphin Cognition and Behavior*, pp. 31-59 (ed. R. J. Schusterman, J. A. Thomas, and F. G. Wood) Lawrence Erlbaum Associates.

Discusses anatomical and physiological characteristics of dolphin brains, including size, convolutedness, cortex volume, metabolism, hemispheric independence, lateralization, and auditory areas.

Seeley, R. L., and J. N. Price 1972 Underwater electric field telemetry of biophysical data. Inst. Electric and Electronic Engr., Region Six Conf. 4 pp.

Describes problems of radiotelemetry of biophysical data from marine mammals, and presents design information which provides solutions to some of these problems.

Seeley, R. L., W. F. Flanigan, Jr., and S. H. Ridgway 1976 A technique for rapidly assessing the hearing of the bottlenosed porpoise, *Tursiops truncatus*. NUC TP 522, 15 pp.

Brainwave activity was used to determine approximate auditory "threshold" levels. This rapid (4-6 hr) technique provides an estimation of the hearing ability of an unanesthetized porpoise over a frequency range of 5 to 200 kHz and could be used to screen hearing in other marine mammals.

Simpson, J. G., W. G. Gilmartin, and S. H. Ridgway 1970 Blood volume and other hematologic values in young elephant seals (*Mirounga angustirostris*). Am. Jour. Vet. Res. *31*(8):1449-1452.

A mean blood volume of 216 ml/kg and a mean packed cell volume of 64% were found. The elephant seal, with the mean blood volume representing 20% or more of body weight, has the highest reported blood volume of any mammal.

31

Simpson, J. G., and M. B. Gardner 1972 Comparative microscopic anatomy of selected marine mammals. In: *Mammals of the Sea - Biology and Medicine*, pp. 298-418 (ed. S. H. Ridgway) Chas. C. Thomas, Publisher.

Profusely illustrated paper on the histology of organs and systems in certain cetaceans and pinnipeds, with emphasis on pathology.

Sweeney, J. C. 1974 Radiographic atlas of the California sea lion. NUC TP 387, 16 pp.

A radiographic reference atlas with an evaluation of techniques for all of the standard positions. Includes photographs and drawings of the normal radiographic anatomy.

Woods, D. L., S. H. Ridgway, and T. H. Bullock 1986 Middle- and long-latency auditory event-related potentials in dolphins. In: *Dolphin Cognition and Behavior*, pp. 61-77 (ed. R. J. Schusterman, J. A. Thomas, and F. G. Wood) Lawrence Erlbaum Associates.

In recordings of event-related potentials in response to a variety of auditory stimuli, certain responses suggested a more precise representation of auditory stimuli in short-term memory in dolphins than in humans. Infrequent "deviant" stimuli produced a component similar in some respects to the "decision-related" P300 wave in humans.

See also Green, Ridgway, and Evans, 1980; and Wood and Evans, 1980, in the SOUND/SONAR/COMMUNICATION section.

3. HEALTH CARE/NUTRITION/PATHOLOGY

Beleau, M. H., and W. G. Gilmartin 1974 Antibiotic serum levels in porpoises. Am Zoo Vets Annual Proceedings, pp. 119-127.

   Serum levels of antibiotics commonly used in porpoises were determined.

Cates, M. B., L. Kaufman, J. H. Grabau, J. M. Pletcher, and J. P. Schroeder 1986 Jour. Am. Vet. Med. Assn *189*:1148-1150.

   A lethargic, anorexic dolphin with a cranial abscess appeared to respond to treatment but died after four weeks. Upon necropsy, *Blastomyces dermatitidis* was found in all major organs.

Cates, M. B., and J. P. Schroeder 1986 The nutrition of acclimated *vs* newly captured *Tursiops truncatus*. Aquatic Mammals *12*:17-20.

   Daily food intake with respect to weight and species of fish fed was recorded as kcal/g of fish dry matter for two groups of dolphins, one in captivity for over six years, the other newly caught in the Gulf of Mexico and transported to Hawaii. The new animals adapted readily to the established feeding regimen.

Colgrove, G. S., T. R. Sawa, J. T. Brown, and P. F. McDowell 1975 Necrotic stomatitis in a dolphin. Jour. Wildlife Diseases *11*:460-464.

   Necrotic stomatitis of undetermined etiology was found in an Atlantic bottlenosed dolphin. The case history, treatment and hematologic findings are described.

Colgrove, G. S. 1975 A survey of *Erysipelothrix insidiosa* agglutinating antibody titres in vaccinated porpoises. Jour. Wildlife Diseases *11*(2):234-236.

   Studies of antibody levels in the blood of porpoises previously vaccinated against the disease.

Colgrove, G. S., and G. Migaki 1976 Cerebral abscess associated with stranding in a dolphin. Jour. Wildlife Diseases *12*:271-274.

   A captive bottlenose dolphin which beached itself in the shallows of its enclosure and later died was found to have an abscess in the right cerebral hemisphere. Examination of the brain revealed a pyogenic meningoencephalitis.

Colgrove, G. S. 1978 Suspected transportation-associated myopathy in a dolphin. Jour. Am. Vet. Med. Assn. *173*(9):1121-1123.

   Evidence suggesting capture myopathy (CM), a potentially fatal condition associated with capture or transport of wildlife, was found in a Pacific bottlenose dolphin following a routine transportation procedure. With treatment the animal recovered. It is speculated that "capture shock" in dolphins may have features in common with CM.

Colgrove, G. S. 1978 Stimulation of lymphocytes from a dolphin (*Tursiops truncatus*) by phytomitogens. Am. Jour. Vet. Res. *39*:141-144.

Dolphin lymphocytes responded (by increased thymidine incorporation) to three phytomitogens, of which one, concanavalin, consistently produced the highest degree of stimulation. Such stimulation could enhance the dolphin's immune response.

Dailey, M. D. 1969 *Stictodora ubelakeri* a new species of heterophylid trematode from the California sea lion (*Zalophus californianus*). Bull. So. Calif. Acad. Sci. *68*(2):82-85.

Describes a new species of parasitic flatworm.

Dailey, M. D., and S. H. Ridgway 1976 A trematode from the round window of an Atlantic bottlenosed dolphin's ear. Jour. Wildlife Diseases *12*:45-47.

A fluke was found attached to the round window of a dolphin's ear. The presence of the fluke could impair hearing.

Dailey, M. D., and W. G. Gilmartin 1980 Diagnostic key to the parasites of some marine mammals. NOSC TD 295, 37 pp.

A key, with illustrations, for identification of parasites of marine mammals studied by the Navy.

DeLong, R. L., W. G. Gilmartin and J. G. Simpson 1973 Premature births in California sea lions: Association with high organochlorine pollutant residual levels. Science *181*:1168-1170.

Organochlorine pesticides and polychlorinated biphenyl residues were two to eight times higher in tissues of premature parturient females and pups than in similar tissues of full-term parturient females and pups collected in 1970.

Diamond, S. S., D. E. Ewing and G. A. Cadwell 1979 Fatal bronchopneumonia and dermatitis caused by *Pseudomonas aeruginosa* in an Atlantic bottlenosed dolphin. Jour. Am. Vet. Med. Assn. *175*(9):984-987.

Diamond, S. S., C. P. Raflo, M. H. Beleau, and G. A. Cadwell 1980 Edema disease in a California sea lion. Jour. Am. Vet. Med. Assn. *177*(9):808-810.

Describes features and identifies probable causative organism of edema disease, similar to that occurring in swine, that was diagnosed in a sea lion.

Gilmartin, W. G., J. F. Allen, and S. H. Ridgway 1971 Vaccination of porpoises (*Tursiops truncatus*) against *Erysipelothrix rhusiopathiae* infection. Jour. Wildlife Diseases *7*:292-295.

A live product was found to stimulate antibody production better than the killed bacterin. An immunization schedule utilizing an initial exposure to the bacterin with subsequent exposures to the live vaccine product is proposed.

Gilmartin, W. G., et al. 1976 Premature parturition in the California sea lion. Jour. Wildlife Diseases *12*:104-114.

The data suggested an interrelationship of disease agents and environmental contaminants as the cause of premature parturition.

Gilmartin, W. G., P. M. Vainik, and V. M. Neill 1979 Salmonellae in feral pinnipeds off the Southern California coast. Jour. Wildlife Diseases *15*:511-514.

Rectal swabs were collected from 90 northern fur seal and 50 California sea lion pups on San Miguel Island. Three Salmonella serotypes were recovered from 33% of the fur seals and 40% of the sea lions.

Hui, C. A., and S. H. Ridgway 1978 Survivorship patterns in captive killer whales *(Orcinus orca)*. Bull. Southern California Acad. Sci. *77*:45-51.

Captive killer whales were found to have an overall mortality rate of 4.7% per year, with females having a higher rate (7%) than males (2.1%), and larger females having a shorter captive life span than smaller females. It is suggested that capture stress may be a significant mortality factor; less stressful capture procedures may increase captive life span.

Johnston, D. G., and S. H. Ridgway 1969 Parasitism in some marine mammals. Jour. Am. Vet. Med. Assn. *155*(7):1064-1072.

Case histories of parasitism in porpoises and sea lions.

Martin, J. H., P. D. Elliott, V. C. Anderlini, D. Girvin, S. A. Jacobs, R. W. Risebrough, R. L. Delong, and W. G. Gilmartin 1976 Mercury-selenium-bromine imbalance in premature parturient California sea lions. In: *Marine Biology*, pp. 91-104. Springer-Verlag, Publ.

Livers and kidneys from 10 normal parturient and 10 premature parturient mothers and their pups were analyzed for 13 trace and major elements. The data suggested a very strong relationship between Hg, Se, and Br in the normal animals but a Br imbalance, in relation to Se and Hg, in the abnormal mothers and their pups. Details and significance of these and other findings are discussed.

Mattsson, J. L., and R. L. Seeley 1974 Simple clinical temperature telemetry system for pinnipeds. Jour. Wildlife Diseases *10*:267-271.

A radiotelemetry pill was used to monitor core body temperature of penned sea lions. Mean core temperature was found to be 38.1° C.

Medway, W., J. G. McCormick, S. H. Ridgway and F. H. Crump 1970 Effects of prolonged halothane anesthesia on some cetaceans. Jour. Am. Vet. Med. Assn. *157*(5):576-582.

After prolonged halothane anesthesia (up to 24 hours) variable histologic changes were found, but were judged not to be significant. Plasma enzyme activities monitored did not indicate significant liver damage.

Migaki, George, R. D. Gunnels, and H. W. Casey 1978 Pulmonary cryptococcosis in an Atlantic bottlenosed dolphin (*Turiops truncatus*). Laboratory Animal Science *28*:603-606.

Pulmonary cryptococcosis was diagnosed in a 7-year-old dolphin that had been in captivity for about 4 years. This was the first report of this disease in a cetacean.

Miller, R. M., and S. H. Ridgway 1963 Clinical experiences with dolphins and whales. Small Animal Clinician *3*(4):189-193.

Diagnosis and treatment of diseases found in dolphins and whales.

Myhre, B. A., J. G. Simpson and S. H. Ridgway 1971 Blood groups in the Atlantic bottlenose porpoise (*Tursiops truncatus*). Proc. Soc. Expl. Biol. Med. *137*:404-407.

A study of porpoise blood demonstrated three blood groups. Transfusions must be made with blood matching that of the recipient.

Ridgway, S. H. 1965 Medical care of marine mammals. Jour. Am. Vet. Med. Assn. *147*(10):1077-1085.

An account of experience gained in the diagnosis and treatment of a variety of marine mammals.

Ridgway, S. H., and D. G. Johnston 1965 Two interesting disease cases in wild cetaceans. Am. Jour. Vet. Res. *26*(112):771-775.

A Pacific common dolphin (*Delphinus*), which stranded itself on a beach, was found to be infested with larval tapeworm cysts, and unidentified ova were found in abscesses in the brain.

Ridgway, S. H., and J. G. Simpson 1967 Anesthesia and restraint for the California sea lion, *Zalophus californianus*. Jour. Am. Vet. Med. Assn. *155*(7):1059-1063.

Describes a technique for anesthetizing sea lions, and the configuration of a unique restraining cage which enables the animal to be examined, treated, or anesthetized without harm to either the sea lion or the handlers.

Ridgway, S. H. 1967 Anesthetization of porpoises for major surgery. Science *158*(3800):510-512.

Account of a technique for achieving deep anesthesia in porpoises. Major surgery (ovario-hysterectomy) has been performed with complete recovery.

Ridgway, S. H. 1968 The bottlenosed dolphin in biomedical research. In: *Methods in Animal Experimentation*. *3*:387-446. (ed. Wm. I. Gay).

A broad account of the characteristics and behavior of the bottlenose dolphin as they relate to health care and biomedical research.

Ridgway, S. H., and J. G. McCormick 1971 Anesthesia of the porpoise. In: *Textbook of Veterinary Anesthesia*, pp. 394-403 (ed. L. R. Soma). The Williams and Wilkins Co., Baltimore.

Discusses special considerations on anesthetizing cetaceans, reviews history of attempts at anesthetization, and describes a successful technique utilizing halothane as the anesthetic.

Ridgway, S. H., and M. D. Dailey 1972 Cerebral and cerebellar involvement of trematode parasites in dolphins and their possible role in stranding. Jour. Wildlife Diseases *8*:33-43.

Trematode parasites found in the brains of stranded porpoises may offer an explanation for some cetacean strandings.

Ridgway, S. H., J. R. Geraci, and W. Medway 1975 Diseases of pinnipeds. Rapp. P.-v. Reun. Cons. Int. Explor. Mer *196*:327-337.

The major disease conditions encountered in pinnipeds are described.

Ridgway, S. H., R. F. Green, and J. C. Sweeney 1975 Mandibular anesthesia and tooth extraction in the bottlenosed dolphin. Jour. Wildlife Diseases *11*:415-418.

Describes a technique for anesthetizing the lower jaw for tooth extraction.

Ridgway, S. H., and J. H. Prescott 1977 The quandary of whether to retain or release rehabilitated strandlings. (Abstract) In: *Biology of Marine Mammals: Insights Through Strandings*, pp. 298-299 (ed. J. B. Geraci and D. J. St. Aubin). Report prepared for Marine Mammal Commission. Nat'l. Tech. Info. Serv. PB-293-890.

Pending availability of information necessary for establishing a release program that will maximize survival of rehabilitated strandlings, the authors recommend that such animals be distributed to public display and research institutions, thereby replacing others that might be taken from wild stocks.

Ridgway, S. H. 1977 Brain abscesses, flukes, and strandings. (Abstract) In: *Biology of Marine Mammals: Insights Through Strandings*, pp. 83-84 (ed. J. B. Geraci and D. J. St. Aubin). Report prepared for Marine Mammal Commission. Nat'l. Tech. Info. Serv. PB-293 890.

Argues that brain abscesses resulting from trematode infestation, which have been found in a number of stranded dolphins, contribute to stranding.

Ridgway, S. H. 1979 Reported causes of death of captive killer whales (*Orcinus orca*). Jour. Wildlife Diseases *15*:99-104.

A variety of diseases and other pathologic conditions were found responsible for deaths of captive killer whales. Captive females appeared to have a higher mortality rate than males. Growth rates for whales that died were greater than for those that survived.

Ridgway, S. H. 1983 Dolphin hearing and sound production in health and illness. In: *Hearing and Other Senses: Presentations in Honor of E. G. Wever*, pp. 247-296 (ed. R. R. Fay and G. Gourevitch), Amphora Press.

Review of findings on dolphin hearing, with accounts of modern anatomic and physiologic work on the ear; the brain, evoked potentials, and audition; and evidence that sound production can be used to assess dolphin health and mood.

Schroeder, J. P., J. G. Wallace, M. B. Greco, and P. W. B. Moore 1985 An infection by *Vibrio alginolyticus* in an Atlantic bottlenose dolphin housed in an open ocean pen. Jour. Wildlife Diseases *21*:437-438.

Describes the lesions on a dolphin that had a history of skin problems, the culture techniques used to identify the pathogen, and the successful therapy following tests to determine sensitivity of the *Vibrio* organisms to a variety of antibiotics. Also discusses the susceptibility of humans to infection by *Vibrio* ssp.

Simpson, J. G., and W. G. Gilmartin 1970 An investigation of elephant seal and sea lion mortality on San Miguel Island. Bioscience, 1 March 1970, p. 289.

At the request of state and federal authorities following the Santa Barbara oil spill, an investigation was made to determine if oil washing up on San Miguel Island had affected any of the seals and sea lions there. No evidence was found of illness or mortality attributable to the oil.

Smith, A. W., C. M. Prato, W. G. Gilmartin, R. J. Brown, and M. C. Keyes 1974 A preliminary report on potentially pathogenic microbiological agents recently isolated from pinnipeds. Jour. Wildlife Diseases *10*:54-59.

Leptospira may be one cause of reproductive failure (abortion) in California sea lions and fur seals. Certain virus isolations from sea lions and fur seals appeared indistinguishable from vesicular exanthoma, a swine virus, which is known to cause abortion in swine. Pinnipeds may constitute a reservoir for virus diseases that infect terrestrial mammals.

Smith, A. W., N. A. Vedros, T. G. Akers, and W. G. Gilmartin 1978 Hazards of disease transfer from marine mammals to land animals: Review and recent findings. Jour. Am. Vet. Med. Assn. *173*:1131-1133.

Certain disease agents, bacterial and viral, are widespread in a variety of marine mammals, and some are transmissible to a number of terrestrial mammal species.

Smith, A. W., and D. E. Skilling 1979 Viruses and virus diseases of marine mammals. Jour. Am. Vet. Med. Assn. *175*:918-920.

Presents information on the kinds of viruses that have been isolated from pinnipeds and cetaceans, and shows, where possible, the relationship of these agents to specific diseases.

Smith, A. W., D. E. Skilling, and Sam Ridgway 1983 Calicivirus-induced vesicular disease in cetaceans and probable interspecies transmission. Jour. Am. Vet. Med. Assn. *183*:1223-1225.

A new calicivirus serotype, isolated from a dolphin, was apparently transmitted from the dolphin to a sea lion and from the sea lion to another dolphin.

Smith, A. W., D. E. Skilling, and S. H. Ridgway 1983 Regression of cetacean tattoo lesions concurrent with conversion of precipitin antibody against a poxvirus. Jour. Am. Vet. Med. Assn. *183*:1219-1222.

Tatoo lesions linked to cetacean poxvirus in bottlenose dolphins regressed without treatment. Regression was concurrent with antibody conversion.

Sweeney, J. C. 1974 Transfusion of homologous and heterologous red blood cells (washed and unwashed) in the California sea lion. Am. Assn. Zoo Vets. Annual Proceedings, pp. 131-135.

Red blood cells tagged with 51_{cr} were used to compare the longevity of homologous and heterologous (sheep) transfused cells. The sheep cells were quickly removed from circulation.

Sweeney, J. C. 1974 Common diseases of pinnipeds. Jour. Am. Vet. Med. Assn. *165*(9):805-810.

Discusses the various diseases found in seals, sea lions, and walruses.

Sweeney, J. C. 1974 Procedures for clinical management of pinnipeds. Jour. Am Vet. Med. Assn. *165*(9):811-814.

Describes clinical approach to diagnoses, treatment techniques, surgical procedures, dietary problems, and physical injuries.

Sweeney, J. C., and W. G. Gilmartin 1974 Survey of diseases in free-living California sea lions. Jour. Wildlife Diseases *10*:370-376.

Presents data on 51 California sea lions that stranded on southern California beaches and were examined by necropsy. Includes comments on the diagnosis and treatment of the more commonly found diseases.

Sweeney, J. C., and S. H. Ridgway 1975 Procedures for the clinical management of small cetaceans. Jour. Am. Vet. Med. Assn. *167*:540-545.

Methods for the treatment of disease and injury in small cetaceans.

Sweeney, J. C., and S. H. Ridgway 1975 Common diseases of small cetaceans. Jour. Am. Vet. Assn. *167*:533-540.

Brief descriptions of commonly encountered disease conditions.

Sweeney, J. C., G. Migaki, P. M. Vainik, and R. H. Conklin 1976 Systemic mycoses in marine mammals. Jour. Am Vet. Med. Assn. *169*(9):946-948.

Thirty-four cases of systemic mycosis were represented by nine genera of fungi. All were characterized by pulmonary involvement.

Sweeney, J. C. 1977 Intratracheal injection of antibiotics in the California sea lion, *Zalophus californianus*, and bottlenose dolphin, *Tursiops truncatus*. Jour. Wildlife Diseases *13*:49-54.

Gentamycin and cephaloridine were administered by intratracheal injections, and uptake and clearance in the blood were monitored. In all cases, absorption through the respiratory mucosa resulted in blood levels approaching therapeutic concentrations despite low dosages.

Van Dyke, D. 1972 Contingency rations for California sea lions. NUC TP 317, 7 pp.

Describes the formulation and testing of a prepared ration that may be fed exclusively for at least 4 weeks.

Van Dyke, D., and S. H. Ridgway 1977 Diets for marine mammals. In: *Handbook of Nutrition and Food*, pp. 595-598 (ed. Miloslav Rechcigl) CRC Press, Cleveland, Ohio.

Diets and caloric intakes of various marine mammals are described.

4. BREEDING

Except as indicated, the following papers are in: *Breeding Dolphins; Present Status, Suggestions for the Future* (ed. S. H. Ridgway and Kurt Benirschke) A report to the Marine Mammal Commission. Nat'l Tech. Info. Serv. PB-273 673, 1977.

Hill, Harold, and W. G. Gilmartin   Collection and storage of semen from dolphins, pp. 205-210.

Discusses relevant considerations and provides details of techniques used.

Hui, C. A.   1975   Growth and physical indices of maturity in the common dolphin, *Delphinus delphis*, pp. 231-260.

Describes growth patterns (as known) in delphinids and discusses the various physical features that provide indication of age or sexual maturity. A "Robustness Quotient" appears to provide a good indicator for female sexual maturity, while a "Flipper Index" (derived from radiographs showing a degree of epiphyseal fusion) provides an estimate of gonad development in males.

Judd, H. L., and S. H. Ridgway   Twenty-four hour patterns of circulating androgens and cortisol in male dolphins, pp. 269-277.

Ultradian and diurnal fluctuations of circulating testosterone were not found in two male *Tursiops* sampled every 20 minutes for 24 hours.

Kirby, V. L., and S. H. Ridgway   1984   Hormonal evidence for spontaneous ovulation of captive dolphins, *Tursiops truncatus* and *Delphinus delphis*. Rep. Int. Whal. Comm. (Special Issue 6): 459-464.

It was concluded that captive females of both species can exhibit spontaneous ovulation; can be anestrous for at least a 1-year period; and can be polyestrous, with an observed maximum of 3 cycles/year for *Tursiops* and 7 cycles/year for *Delphinus*.

Leatherwood, J. S.   Some preliminary impressions on the numbers and social behavior of free-swimming bottlenosed dolphin calves (*Tursiops truncatus*) in the northern Gulf of Mexico, pp. 143-167.

Data from aerial observations on numbers of calves observed with respect to (1) positions within herds of subgroups containing calves, (2) positions of calves within subgroups, (3) interactions between calves and other animals in the herd, and (4) changes in the behavior of calves with age. Apparent patterns were seen. Relevant observations from other field and captive studies are discussed.

Ridgway, S. H., and R. F. Green   1967   Evidence for a sexual rhythm in male porpoises. Norwegian Whaling Gazette No. 1, pp. 1-8.

Describes seasonal changes in the reproductive organs of two species of porpoises.

Sweeney, J. C. Difficult births and neonatal health problems in small cetaceans, pp. 278-287.

> Analysis of records of stillbirths, difficulties in labor (dystocias), and neonatal health problems and mortalities, with conclusions and recommendations.

Sweeney, J. C. Diagnosis of pregnancy in small cetaceans with Doppler sonography and other techniques, pp. 211-216.

> Discusses electronic devices and various techniques by which pregnancy and fetal viability can be determined.

Wood, F. G. Births of porpoises at Marineland, Florida, 1939-1969, and comments on problems in captive breeding of small Cetacea, pp. 47-60.

> Discusses behavioral factors, births to captive-born females, time of year births occurred, stillbirths, and infant mortalities, with relevant tables, including a listing of 40 births with dates, sex of calf, name of dam, place of conception (ocean or tank), parturition time, and additional details.

5. BEHAVIOR/PSYCHOPHYSICS

Beach, F. A., III, and R. L. Pepper 1971 Marine mammal training procedures: The effects of scheduled reinforcement in the dolphin (*Tursiops truncatus*). NUC TP 214, 72 pp.

The strength of a behavior conditioned on a one-reward-for-one-response basis was compared with that conditioned on several types of schedules in which more than one response was required for a reward. All schedules provided good control, but a variable-ratio schedule produced a larger amount of work over a longer period and at a greater rate for the same amount of reward.

Beach, F. A., III, and L. M. Herman 1972 Preliminary studies of auditory problem solving and intertask transfer by the bottlenose dolphin. Psych. Rec. 22:49-62.

Describes successive reversal training and discrimination learning set experiments with two bottlenose dolphins.

Beach, F. A., III, and R. L. Pepper 1972 Operant responding in the bottlenose dolphin (*Tursiops truncatus*). Jour. Exper. Anal. Behavior 17(2):159-160.

Describes experiments to determine the relative efficacies of various food-reinforcement schedules in a paddle-press task.

Beach, F. A., III, R. L. Pepper, J. V. Simmons, Jr., P. E. Nachtingall, and P. A. Siri 1974 Spatial habit reversal in two species of marine mammals. Psyche. Rec. 24:385-391.

Two California sea lions and one Atlantic bottlenose dolphin were tested over 19 reversals of a spatial problem. All performed well.

Chun, N. K. W. 1978 Aerial visual shape discrimination and matching-to-sample problem solving ability of an Atlantic bottlenose dolphin. NOSC TR 236, 24 pp.

Two-dimensional geometric shapes of various configurations were presented. Large differences in perimeter lengths between any two shapes generally resulted in better performance. Other form parameters may be involved in the discriminative process. Evidence indicated problem-specific rather than conceptual learning.

Cummings, W. C., P. O. Thompson and J. F. Fish 1974 Behavior of southern right whales: R/V Hero cruise 72-3. Antarctic Jour. U.S. 9(2):33-38.

Describes behaviors and underwater sounds of right whales in Golfo San Jose, Argentina. No decided change in behavior was elicited by playback of southern right whale sounds or the sounds of northeast Pacific killer whales.

Flanigan, W. F., Jr. 1974 Nocturnal behavior of captive small cetaceans. 2. The beluga whale, *Delphinapterus leucas*. Sleep Research 3:85 (Abstract).

Observed behavior consisted of active waking, quiet waking, and stereotypic circular swimming. The last does not meet all the criteria used to define sleep in terrestrial animals but probably reflects adaptations to an aquatic environment.

Flanigan, W. P., Jr. 1974 Nocturnal behavior of captive small cetaceans. 1. The bottlenosed porpoise, *Tursiops truncatus*. Sleep Research *3*:84 (Abstract).

Observed behavior consisted of periods of unambiguous waking, stereotypic circular swimming with brief (20-30 sec) eye closure and other indications of sleep, and quiescent "hanging" behavior with similar indications of sleep.

Haun, J. E. 1977 Trainer and trainer transfer of marine mammals utilizing collateral behaviors. In: *Proceedings of the International Marine Trainers Association Conference*, pp. 65-79 (ed. Don McSheehy and Gail Peiterson) New England Aquarium, Boston, MA.

Discusses the classification and quantification of innovative or animal-initiated behaviors that occur in performance of a conditioned chain of behaviors and describes how such collateral behaviors pertain to training and can be used to facilitate transfer of an animal from one trainer to another.

Irvine, Blair 1971 (1972) Behavior changes in dolphins in a strange environment. Quart. Jour. Florida Acad. Sci. *34*(3):206-212.

Sluggish and unresponsive behavior was observed in dolphins when they were first moved from tanks to lagoon pens. Similar behavior was noted in animals that escaped from their pens or wandered away from the trainer during early training. It is suggested that this was a response to a strange environment.

Leatherwood, J. S. 1974 Aerial observations of migrating gray whales, *Eschrichtius robustus*, off Southern California, 1969-1972. Mar. Fish. Rev. *36*(4):45-49.

Presents data on movements, numbers, and distance from offshore, with details as to cows with calves and yearling animals observed.

Leatherwood, J. S. 1974 A note on gray whale behavioral interactions with other marine mammals. Mar. Fish. Rev. *36*(4):50-51.

Porpoises of a number of species were observed riding the pressure waves of the whales. Whales were also observed riding large swells in a manner similar to that seen in smaller cetaceans.

Leatherwood, Stephen 1975 Some observations of feeding behavior of bottlenosed dolphins (*Tursiops truncatus*) in the northern Gulf of Mexico and (*Tursiops cf. T. gilli*) off Southern California, Baja California, and Nayarit, Mexico. Mar. Fish. Rev. *37*(9):10-16.

Seven distinct feeding behaviors, in which a variety of prey species are taken by various means, are identified and discussed.

Leatherwood, Stephen, D. K. Ljungblad   1979   Nighttime swimming and diving behavior of a radio-tagged spotted dolphin, *Stenella attenuata*.   Cetology, No. 34, 6 pp.

The dolphin, radio-tracked from shipboard for 13 consecutive hours, covered 100.5 km at estimated speeds of 2.3 to 10.7 knots, with burst speeds exceeding 12 knots. The animal dived for from 1 to 204 seconds, exhibiting three diving modes tentatively identified as running, traveling, and feeding.

Ljungblad, D. K., and S. E. Moore   1983   Killer whales (*Orcinus orcus*) chasing gray whales (*Eschrichtius robustus*) in the northern Bering Sea.   Arctic 36:361-364.

Behaviors observed when 16 killer whales approached and chased feeding gray whales. No whale sounds were picked up by a sonobuoy although widely spaced killer whales exhibited apparently coordinated movements.

Murchison, A. E., and R. L. Pepper   1972   Escape conditioning in the bottlenose dolphin (*Tursiops truncatus*)   Cetology No. 8, 5 pp.

In order to evaluate the effectiveness of procedures other than food reward in establishing behavioral control, the use of an aversive stimulus was investigated. The animal was successfully conditioned to approach an emitting hydrophone in order to terminate the presentation of a moderately intense sound delivered underwater.

Nachtigall, P. E.   1971   Spatial discrimination and reversal based on differential magnitude of reward in the dolphin *Tursiops truncatus*.   Proc. 8th Ann. Conf. Biol. Sonar and Diving Mammals, pp. 67-72, Stanford Research Institute, Menlo Park, California.

Tursiops responds to differential reward magnitudes (four smelt versus one smelt) in a manner characteristic of other animals similarly studied.

Pepper, R. L., and F. A. Beach, III,   1972   Deprivation and other aspects of food reinforcement in the dolphin.   Proc. 9th Conf. Biol. Sonar and Diving Animals, 10 pp.

Dolphin behavior in a simple automated task was found to be responsive to controlled variations in food reinforcement.

Pepper, R. L., and F. A. Beach, III   1972   Preliminary investigations of tactile reinforcement in the dolphin.   Cetology No. 7, 8 pp.

Tactile reinforcement, gradually substituted for fish in a paddle-press task, at first maintained good response. After extensive testing, behavioral breakdown occurred. Aggressive behavior directed toward the trainer was interpreted as sexual frustration.

Pepper, R. L., and R. H. Defran 1975 Dolphin Trainers Handbook, Part 1. Basic Training. NUC TP 432, 52 pp.

> A handbook of information and guidance for dolphin trainers.

Schusterman, R. J. 1981 Behavioral capabilities of seals and sea lions: A review of their hearing, visual, learning, and diving skills. Psych. Rec. *31*:125-143.

> Compares behavioral/sensory capabilities of otariids (fur seals and sea lions) and phocids (earless seals).

Wood, F. G., D. K. Caldwell and M. C. Caldwell 1970 Behavioral interactions between porpoises and sharks. In: *Investigations on Cetacea*, Vol. II, pp. 264-279 (ed. G. Pilleri) Institute of Brain Anatomy, Berne, Switzerland.

> Sometimes porpoises attack sharks, sometimes sharks attack (and eat) porpoises, and sometimes mutual tolerance is exhibited. The relationship of porpoises and sharks is still inadequately understood.

Wood, F. G. 1986 Social behavior and foraging strategies of dolphins. (Section introduction) In: *Dolphin Cognition and Behavior*, pp. 331-333 (ed. R. J. Schusterman, J. A. Thomas, and F. G. Wood) Lawrence Erlbaum Associates.

> Dolphin social and feeding behaviors, first observed in oceanariums, have now been studied in free-ranging animals. While conditions of captivity may distort natural patterns, observations of behavior of captive animals can be useful in interpreting that of free-living dolphins. Captive conditions appear to stimulate dolphin propensities for play and the invention of games.

See also Nachtigall and Patterson 1980 in the SOUND/SONAR/COMMUNICATION section.

6. OPEN SEA RELEASE

Bailey, R. E. 1965 Training and open sea release of an Atlantic bottlenose porpoise *Tursiops truncatus* (Montagu). NOTS TP 3838, 17 pp.

Describes the first open water release of a trained porpoise.

Bowers, C. A., and R. S. Henderson 1972 Project Deep Ops: Deep object recovery with pilot and killer whales. NUC TP 306, 86 pp.

Killer whales and pilot whales were conditioned to locate and mark or recover cylindrical objects containing acoustic beacons which had been placed on the ocean floor. The two killer whales deployed practice recovery devices at maximum depths of 500 and 850 feet. A pilot whale deployed the device at 1654 feet, and on one occasion apparently made a volunteered dive (without the device) to 2000 feet.

Conboy, M. E. 1972 Project Quick Find: A marine mammal system for object recovery. NUC TP 268, Rev. 1, 31 pp.

Sea lions were trained to attach a nosecup-mounted grabber device to "pingered" objects on the ocean floor so that the objects (e.g. test ordnance, oceanographic instruments) can then be hauled to the surface by a line attached to the grabber. The system has been demonstrated to depths of 500 feet.

Evans, W. E., and S. R. Harmon 1968 Experimenting with trained pinnipeds in the open sea. In: *The Behavior and Physiology of Pinnipeds*, pp. 196-208 (ed. R. J. Harrison et al.) Appleton-Century-Crofts.

Details training procedures and results of deep-diving studies using seals and sea lions.

Hall, J. D. 1970 Conditioning Pacific white-striped dolphins, *Lagenorhynchus obliquidens*, for open-ocean release. NUC TP 200, 14 pp.

Pacific white-striped dolphins were for the first time trained for open sea release.

Irvine, B. 1970 Conditioning marine mammals to work in the sea. Marine Tech. Soc. Jour. 4(3):47-52.

Describes training procedures for open sea release.

Marcus, S. R. 1972 Turk, the sea lion, helps the Navy: Project Quick Find. Naval Ordnance Bulletin, March 1972, pp. 36-39.

A nontechnical article on the recovery of an instrumented ASROC depth charge by a sea lion. See Conboy reference above.

Ridgway, S. H. 1966 Studies on diving depth and duration in Tursiops truncatus. Proc. 1966 Conf. Biol. Sonar and Diving Mammals, 151-158. Stanford Research Institute, Menlo Park, California.

Describes technique by which a bottlenose porpoise was trained to dive to depths down to 550 feet and perform other tasks in preparation for participation in Sealab II. Total dive time to 550 feet and back averaged 163 seconds.

Ridgway, S. H. 1969 Sea lion recovery float. NUC TP 134, 5 pp.

To prevent sea lions from diving and swimming away during open sea training, a gas-generator float was developed employing a water-soluble washer as a timer and release mechanism, and a small balloon for flotation.

Wood, F. G., and S. H. Ridgway 1967 Utilization of porpoises in the Man-In-The-Sea Program. In: *ONR Report ACR-124, An Experimental 45-Day Undersea Saturation Dive at 205 feet*, pp. 407-411.

At Sealab II a bottlenose dolphin named Tuffy was trained to carry objects between the surface and aquanauts working on the ocean floor. He also demonstrated his ability to carry a line from the habitat to a "lost" aquanaut. The conditioning of Tuffy and details of his transports to and from the Sealab site are described.

7. TAGGING/TELEMETRY/SURVEYS

Clarke, J. T., S. E. Moore, and D. K. Ljungblad 1987 Observations of bowhead whale (*Balaena mysticetus*) calves in the Alaskan Beaufort Sea during the autumn migration, 1982-85. Rep. Int. Whal. Comm. *37*:287-293.

Analysis of sightings of 44 calves by geographic location, month, presence of adults, behavior, and ice cover.

Evans, W. E. 1970 Uses of advanced space technology and upgrading the future of oceanography. AIAA Paper No. 7-01273, 3 pp.

Two species of small whales equipped with small radio-telemetry packages so that their movements could be tracked have provided information on the animals' physical environment as a function of depth. Further data have been derived on areas of high biologic productivity and underwater topographical features. Telemetering via satellite would greatly extend the utility of this technique to oceanography.

Evans, W. E. 1971 Orientation behavior of delphinids: radio-telemetric studies. In: *Orientation: Sensory Basis*, pp. 142-160 (ed. H. E. Adler) Annals New York Acad. Sci., Vol. 188.

The movements and diving behavior of wild common dolphins (*Delphinus delphis*) were ascertained by means of small radio transmitters attached to the animals.

Evans, W. E., and J. S. Leatherwood 1972 The use of an instrumented marine mammal as an oceanographic survey platform. NUC TP 331, 11 pp.

By a small radio transmitter attached to its dorsal fin, a *Delphinus* was tracked for 3 days. The radio signal, transmitted when the dolphin surfaced, provided data on duration and depth of dives, and indicated probable nocturnal feeding on organisms of the deep scattering layer at depths to 846 feet.

Evans, W. E., J. D. Hall, A. B. Irvine, and J. S. Leatherwood 1972 Methods for tagging small cetaceans. Fishery Bulletin *70*(1):61-65.

Describes tests of four techniques for tagging delphinids: plastic button tags, spaghetti tags, radio tags, and freeze branding.

Hui, C. A. 1979 Undersea topography and distribution of dolphins of the genus *Delphinus* in the Southern California Bight. Jour. Mamm. *60*:521-527.

Delphinus occurs more frequently in areas of high relief. Availability of prey species over areas of different relief may be a major factor influencing distribution patterns. Herd size is greater (median 250) from May to October when anchovies are the major diet component; from November to April the median aggregation size is 40.

Leatherwood, Stephen, J. R. Gilbert, and D. G. Chapman 1978 An evaluation of some techniques for aerial censuses of bottlenosed dolphins. Jour. Wildlife Management 42:239-250.

Discusses field procedures and analytical techniques based on surveys conducted off the coasts of Louisiana, Mississippi, and Alabama. Population estimates from strip censuses are given for several areas, and suggestions are made for future censuses of dolphins inhabiting inshore waters.

Leatherwood, Stephen, L. J. Harrington-Coulombe, and C. L. Hubbs 1978 Relict survival of the sea otter in Central California and evidence of its recent redispersal south of Point Conception. Bull. Southern California Acad. Sci. 77:109-115.

Details the past distribution of the sea otter; its apparent extirpation south of Alaska; the discovery of a remnant population in Monterey County, California, which has since proliferated; and recent sightings south of Point Conception.

Leatherwood, Stephen 1979 Aerial survey of the bottlenosed dolphin, Tursiops truncatus, and the West Indian manatee, Trichechus manatus, in the Indian and Banana Rivers, Florida. Fish Bull. 77:47-59.

The population of dolphins in the rivers during the week of the survey (10-15 Aug 1977) was estimated to be 438 ± 127. There were 60 sightings of manatees totaling 151 animals; no attempt was made to estimate the size of the manatee population.

Ljungblad, D. K. 1981 Aerial surveys of endangered whales in the Beaufort Sea, Chukchi Sea, and northern Bering Sea. NOSC TD 449, 302 pp.

Describes aerial surveys and acoustic recordings of bowhead whales and other marine mammals from April to November 1980. Ice conditions radically altered the migration pattern seen in 1979.

Ljungblad, D. K., S. E. Moore, D. R. Van Schoik, and C. S. Winchell 1982 Aerial surveys of endangered whales in the Beaufort, Chukchi, and northern Bering Seas. NOSC TD 486, 374 pp.

Aerial surveys, acoustic recordings, and behavioral observations of bowhead whales were made prior to and during the spring migration and again during the fall migration. Summer survey efforts concentrated on gray whale distribution and behavior.

Ljungblad, D. K. 1983 Interaction between offshore geophysical exploration activities and bowhead whales in the Alaskan Beaufort Sea, Fall 1982. Jour. Acoust. Soc. Am. Vol. 74, Suppl. 1, p. S55.

Aerial surveys, supplemented by the use of sonobuoys, revealed no major changes in the behavior of bowheads exposed to seismic exploration sounds.

Ljungblad, D. K., S. E. Moore, and D. R. Van Schoik 1984 Aerial surveys of endangered whales in the northern Bering, eastern Chukchi, and Alaskan Beaufort Seas, 1983: With a 5-year review, 1979-1983. NOSC TR 995, 370 pp.

Presents survey results and observations on bowhead distribution, relative abundance, migration patterns, general behavior, and sound production. Includes survey results and observations on gray whale distribution, relative abundance, and general behavior for July.

Ljungblad, D. K., S. E. Moore, J. T. Clarke, D. R. Van Schoik, and J. C. Bennett 1985 Aerial surveys of endangered whales in the northern Bering, eastern Chukchi, and Alaskan Beaufort Seas, 1984: With a six year review, 1979-1984. NOSC TR 1046. 302 pp. incl. appendices.

Ljungblad, D. K., S. E. Moore, J. T. Clarke, and J. C. Bennett 1986 Aerial surveys of endangered whales in the northern Bering, eastern Chukchi, and Alaskan Beaufort Seas, 1985: With a seven year review, 1979-85. NOSC TR 1111, 407 pp. incl. appendices.

Both of the above items present survey results and observations on bowhead distribution, relative abundance, migration patterns, general behavior, and sound production for spring and fall months. Survey results and observations on gray whale distribution, relative abundance, and general behavior are also included, along with sightings of other marine mammals.

Ljungblad, D. K., S. E. Moore, and J. T. Clarke 1986 Assessment of bowhead whale (*Balaena mysticetus*) feeding patterns in the Alaskan Beaufort and northeastern Chukchi Seas via aerial surveys, Fall 1979-84. Rep. Int. Whal. Comm. *36*:265-272.

Feeding bowheads occurred in larger groups, in shallower water, and in lighter ice cover than nonfeeding whales. Among feeding whales, differences in group size at different locations and in feeding patterns may have been due to the type of prey and its distribution, abundance, and location in the water column.

Ljungblad, D. K., S. E. Moore, D. R. Van Schoik 1986 Seasonal patterns of distribution, abundance, migration and behavior of the western arctic stock of bowhead whales, *Balaena mysticetus*, in Alaskan seas. Rep. Int. Whal. Comm. Special Issue *8*:177-205.

A detailed analysis of sightings during spring and fall months between 1979 and 1983.

Ljungblad, D. K., S. E. Moore, J. T. Clarke, and J. C. Bennett 1987 Distribution, abundance, behavior, and bioacoustics of endangered whales in the Alaskan Beaufort and eastern Chukchi Seas, 1979-86. NOSC TR 1177, 362 pp. incl. appendices.

Report covers survey results and observations on bowhead distribution, relative abundance and density, migration patterns, general behavior, and sound production recorded from air-dropped sonobuoys and from a station established on Barter Island. Survey results and observations on gray whale distribution, relative abundance, and general behavior are included, along with incidental sightings of other marine mammals.

Moore, S. E., and D. K. Ljungblad 1984 Gray whales in the Beaufort, Chukchi, and Bering Seas: Distribution and sound production. In: *The Gray Whale*, pp. 543-559 (ed. M. L. Jones, S. L. Schwartz, and S. Leatherwood), Academic Press.

Gray whale occurrence, distribution, behavior, and sound production were studied during aerial surveys in arctic waters in 1980 and 1981.

Moore, S. E., J. T. Clarke, and D. K. Ljungblad 1986 A comparison of gray whale (*Eschrichtius robustus*) and bowhead whale (*Balaena mysticetus*) distribution, abundance, habitat preference and behavior in the northeastern Chukchi Sea, 1982-1984. Rep. Int. Whal. Comm. *36*:273-279.

On aerial surveys conducted from July to October, differences between the two species were observed with respect to distance from shore, in open water *vs.* near ice cover, shallowness of water, and incidence of feeding behavior.

Moore, S. E., D. K. Ljungblad, and D. R. Van Schoik 1986 Annual patterns of gray whale (*Eschrichtius robustus*) distribution, abundance, and behavior in the northern Bering and eastern Chukchi Seas, July 1980-83. Rep. Int. Whal. Comm. Special Issue *8*:231-242.

Analysis of sightings, in the course of aerial surveys, of 1,543 gray whales with respect to distribution, estimated gross annual recruitment rate, behaviors, and sound production.

Reeves, R. R., D. K. Ljungblad, and J. T. Clarke 1984 Bowhead whales and acoustic seismic surveys in the Beaufort Sea. Polar Record *22*(138):270-280.

Seismic survey activities were monitored in autumn 1982 for their possible effects on migrating bowheads. Distribution, behavior, and numbers of whales were recorded; one possible behavioral response to seismic shooting was observed.

Richardson, W. J., R. A. Davis, C. R. Evans, D. K. Ljungblad, and Pamela Norton 1987 Summer distribution of bowhead whales, *Balaena mysticetus*, relative to oil industry activities in the Canadian Beaufort Sea, 1980-84. Arctic *40*(2):93-104.

Distribution of bowheads both outside and within the "main industrial area" varied from year to year. Their numbers decreased, whether from increasing industrial activity or from variations in the whales' zooplankton prey is not clear.

Sweeney, J. C., and J. L. Mattsson 1974 Surgical attachment of a telemetry device to the dorsal ridge of a yearling California gray whale, *Eschrichtius robustus*. Mar. Fish. Rev. *36*(4):20-22.

Describes technique by which an instrument package-mounting device was attached to the whale.

8. HYDRODYNAMICS

Haun, J. E., E. W. Hendricks, F. R. Borkat, R. W. Kataoka, D. A. Carder, and N. K. Chun 1983 Dolphin hydrodynamics annual report F.Y. 82. NOSC TR 935, 82 pp.

Describes various studies undertaken in the course of an investigation of the hydrodynamic characteristics of dolphins.

Hui, C. A. 1987 Power and speed of swimming dolphins. Jour. Mamm. *68*:126-132.

Analysis of measured swimming speeds for dolphins of the *Stenella-Delphinus* morphology, using a conservative hydrodynamics model and a metabolic rate 13.4 times the projected resting metabolic rate, indicated that energy expenditure was entirely within expected ranges and no extraordinary mechanisms are necessary to explain observations.

Lang, T. G. 1963 Porpoise, whales and fish: Comparison of predicted and observed speeds. Naval Engineers Jour. May 1963, pp. 437-441.

Concludes that reported speeds of cetaceans and fish can be explained by an unusual extent of laminar flow.

Lang, T. G., and D. A. Daybell 1963 Porpoise performance tests in a seawater tank. NOTS TP 3063, 50 pp.

A hydrodynamic study conducted with a trained *Lagenorhynchus obliquidens* in a long seawater tank revealed no unusual physiological or hydrodynamic phenomena. Because the tank conditions may have affected the animal's performance, further tests in the open sea were recommended.

Lang, T. G., and K. S. Norris 1966 Swimming speed of a Pacific bottlenose porpoise. Science *151*:588-590.

See next item.

Lang, T. G., and K. S. Pryor 1966 Hydrodynamic performance of porpoises. *(Stenella attenuata)*. Science *152*:531-533.

The above two papers describe open-ocean speed runs of trained porpoises. Top speeds recorded were 16.1 knots (*Tursiops gilli*) and 21.4 knots (*Stenella attenuata*). The results compared closely with highest predictions based on rigid-body drag calculations and estimated available power output.

Lang, T. G. 1966 Hydrodynamic analysis of cetacean performance. In: *Whales, Dolphins, and Porpoises*, pp. 410-432 (ed. K. S. Norris) U. of Calif. Press.

A detailed discussion of cetacean hydrodynamic performance, presented at the First International Symposium on Cetacean Research held in Washington, DC in August 1963.

Lang, T. G. 1966 Hydrodynamic analysis of dolphin fin profiles. Nature 209:110-111.

Cross sections of dolphin fins were found to have a shape intermediate between two independently proposed hydrodynamic shapes believed to have superior characteristics.

Madigosky, W. M., G. F. Lee, J. Haun, F. Borkat, and R. Kataoka 1983 Acoustic surface wave measurements on live bottlenose dolphins. NSWC TR 83-312, 18 pp.

In connection with a hydrodynamics study, dolphin skin properties were measured by determining responses to acoustic surface waves generated at different locations on the dolphins.

9. MISCELLANEOUS

Blanchard, R. E. 1975 Development of a selection procedure for marine mammal trainers. NUC TP 490, 70 pp.

Describes a program of personnel research leading to a selection procedure for marine mammal trainers.

Bowers, C. A., and R. E. Austin 1983 Capture, transport, and initial adaptation of beluga whales. NOSC TR 811, 16 pp.

Describes techniques used in the capture, transport, and handling and feeding of six belugas, three captured in 1977 and three in 1980. The first three took over 3 months to complete adaptation. The second three, which benefited from techniques developed with the first group, reached the same stage in less than 2 months.

Duffield, D. A., S. H. Ridgway and R. S. Sparkes 1967 Cytogenetic studies of two species of porpoise. Nature *213*(5072):189-190.

The diploid chromosome number for a male and female *Tursiops truncatus* and for two males and one female *Lagenorhynchus obliquidens* was found to be 44. There were no obvious differences in the karyotypes of the two species.

Duffield, D. A., S. H. Ridgway, and L. H. Cornell 1983 Hematology distinguishes coast and offshore forms of dolphins (*Tursiops*). Can. Jour. Zool. *61*:930-933.

Bottlenose dolphins can be separated into coastal and offshore ecotypes based on hematologic values, the offshore forms having higher values. There appears to be a significant genetic basis for these differences.

Hall, J. D., W. G. Gilmartin, and J. L. Mattsson 1971 Investigation of a Pacific pilot whale stranding on San Clemente Island. Jour. Wildlife Diseases *7*:324-327.

From a stranding of 28 pilot whales, information was obtained on their bacteriology, reproductive tissue, histopathology, and liver mercury and DDE levels. It was concluded that the stranding was a natural event, not precipitated by any pathological condition.

Herald, E. S. 1969 A field and aquarium study of the blind river dolphin (Platanista gangetica). NUC TP 153, 62 pp.

Blind river dolphins ("susu") from the Indus River of Pakistan swim on their sides. Presumably this permits a lateral echolocation sweep of the bottom. Underwater sound emissions of pulse trains are produced continuously.

Hui, C. A. 1985 Undersea topography and the comparative distributions of two pelagic cetacean. Fish. Bull. *83*:472-475.

The daytime distributions of pilot whales and common dolphins in the California Bight were found to be similar above undersea topography of high relief, but common dolphins occurred more frequently over areas of low relief. Differences in the distributions may be due to different foraging strategies.

Irvine, B. 1970 An inflatable porpoise pen. NUC TP 181, 10 pp.

An inflatable, readily portable porpoise pen was designed, constructed, and tested in the open sea.

Kulu, Deborah D., Iris Veomett, and R. S. Sparkes 1971 Cytogenetic comparison of four species of cetaceans. Jour. Mamm. *52*(4):828-832.

The model chromosome number for the common dolphin, Amazon freshwater dolphin, Dall's porpoise, and killer whale is 44, the same as that in other cetaceans examined, with the exception of the sperm whale, which has 42. Karyotypes of the killer and sperm whales are otherwise similar. The possible significance of these findings is discussed.

Leatherwood, J. S., W. E. Evans and D. W. Rice 1972 *The Whales, Dolphins, and Porpoises of the Eastern North Pacific; A Guide to Their Identification in the Water.* NUC TP 282, 175 pp.

A key, with descriptions and illustrations, of cetaceans found in the eastern North Pacific Ocean.

Leatherwood, J. S., R. A. Johnson, D. K. Ljungblad, and W. E. Evans 1977 Broadband measurements of underwater acoustic target strengths of panels of tuna nets. NOSC TR 126, 18 pp.

Target strengths of sample panels of tuna nets of three different mesh sizes were determined. All panels produced sufficiently strong returns to allow porpoises to detect them acoustically.

Leatherwood, Stephen, and D. W. Beach 1975 A California gray whale calf *Eschrictius robustus* born outside the calving lagoons. S. Calif. Acad. Sci. Bull. *74*(1):45-46.

The birth of a living calf was observed off San Diego, far north of the lagoons where calving normally occurs.

Leatherwood, Stephen, D. K. Caldwell and H. E. Winn 1976 *Whales, Dolphins and Porpoises of the Western North Atlantic.* NOAA Tech. Rept. NMFS CIRC-396, 1972 pp.

A field guide to permit identification of cetaceans seen in the western North Atlantic, including the Caribbean Sea, the Gulf of Mexico, and coastal waters of the U.S. and Canada. Includes a key to aid in identification of stranded cetaceans, as well as appendices telling to whom to report data on live and dead cetaceans.

Ridgway, S. H., N. J. Flanagan, and J. G. McCormick 1966 Brain-spinal cord ratio in porpoises: Possible correlations with intelligence and ecology. Psychon. Sci., 6(11):491-492.

It has been suggested that brain weight:spinal cord weight ratios may provide a rough index of intelligence in vertebrate animals. This ratio in the bottlenose porpoise average 40:1, as compared to the 50:1 ratio in man.

Ridgway, S. H. 1966 Dall porpoise, *Phocaenoides dalli* (True): Observations in captivity and at sea. Norwegian Whaling Gazette No. 5, pp. 97-110.

Describes the natural history, capture, recorded sounds, and anatomy of Dall's porpoises, three of which were maintained at the Navy's Marine Bioscience Facility for periods ranging from 26 days to 10 months. No members of this species had previously survived in capacity.

Ridgway, S. H., and R. J. Harrison, Eds. 1981 Handbook of Marine Mammals, Vol. 1: The Walrus, Sea Lions, Fur Seals, and Sea Otter. xvi +236 pp. Academic Press.

Ridgway, S. H., and R. J. Harrison, Eds. 1981 Handbook of Marine Mammals, Vol. 2: Seals. xiv +364 pp. Academic Press.

Ridgway, S. H., and R. J. Harrison, Eds. 1985 Handbook of Marine Mammals, Vol. 3: The Sirenians and Baleen Whales. xv +362 pp. Academic Press.

In the above volumes, chapters on the various species include taxonomy, evolution, morphology and anatomy, abundance and life history, behavior, reproduction and diseases. (Although not derived from the Navy's Marine Mammal Program, these works are included because senior editor Ridgway drew on the extensive knowledge gained from his participation in the Program since its inception.)

Ridgway, S. H., and C. C. Robison 1985 Homing by released captive California sea lions, *Zalophus californianus*, following release on distant islands. Can. Jour. Zool. 63:2162-2164.

Three sea lions returned to their pen in San Diego Bay after being released on San Clemente Island, about 115 km away. Two of four returned from San Nicholas Island, some 240 km away. Times for the fastest animal were 2 days and 4 days respectively.

Squire, Ina 1964 A bibliography of Cetacea: Literature published between 1949 and 1963. NOTS TP 3686, 118 pp.

Steele, J. W. 1971 Marine-environment cetacean holding and training enclosures. NUC TP 227, 25 pp.

Describes construction details of three types of marine holding facilities for cetaceans: a permanent wood piling and galvanized-wire fencing enclosure, a permanent concrete-steel piling and fencing enclosure, and a floating pen supported by steel drums.

Wood, F. G. 1973 Marine Mammals and Man: *The Navy's Porpoises and Sea Lions*. R. B. Luce, Publishers, Washington, D.C. 264 pp.

A nontechnical account of the Navy's marine mammal program, with considerable background information on porpoises. Topics include capture and care, sonar, intelligence and communication, deep diving, hydrodynamics, and open ocean work.

Wood, F. G. 1979 The cetacean stranding phenomenon: A hypothesis. In: *Biology of Marine Mammals: Insights Through Strandings*, pp. 129-188 (ed. J. B. Geraci and D. J. St. Aubin), Report prepared for Marine Mammal Commission. Nat'l. Tech. Info. Serv. PB-293 890.

Discusses previous explanations of live strandings, presents stranding data, details circumstances of many strandings, and proposes that stranding may be attributed to a subcortical response to stress originating in amphibious ancestors and persisting to this day, despite its apparently maladaptive nature.

END
Feb.
1988
DTIC

www.ingramcontent.com/pod-product-compliance
Lightning Source LLC
Chambersburg PA
CBHW081258170426
43198CB00017B/2839